A HISTORY OF ART

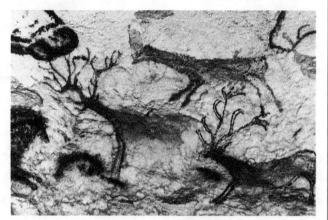

Cave painting, Lascaux, France, 15,000–10,000 B.C.

The RANDOM HOUSE
LIBRARY OF KNOWLEDGE™

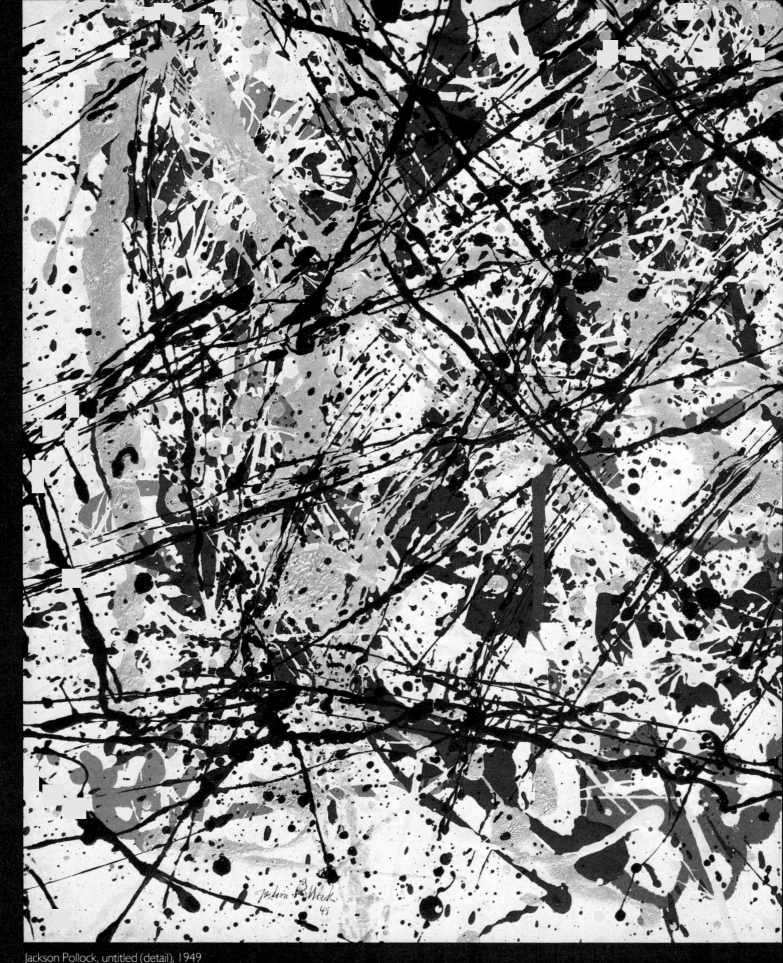

Jackson Pollock, untitled (detail), 1949

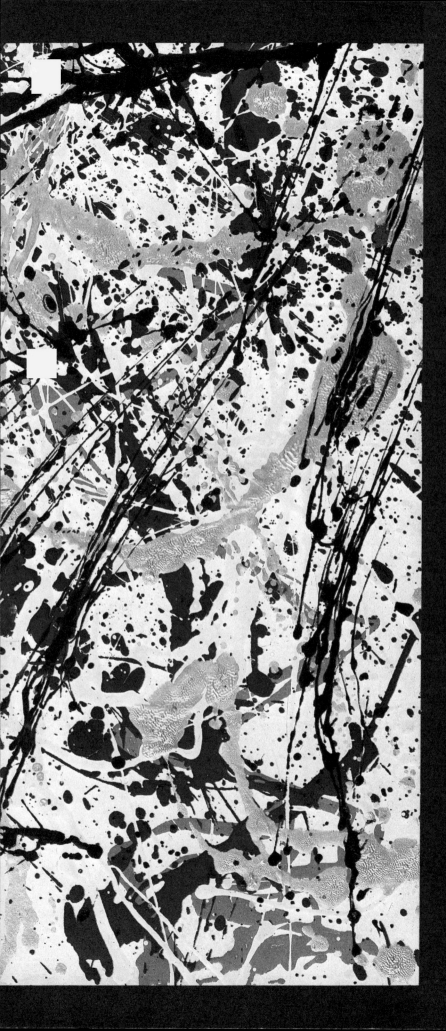

A HISTORY OF ART

From 25,000 B.C. to the Present

by Marshall B. Davidson

RANDOM HOUSE
NEW YORK

Grateful acknowledgment is made to the following for permission to reproduce the works illustrated:

T = top, M = middle, B = bottom, R = right, L = left.

Anderson / Alinari / Art Resource: p. 49 BR; Art Institute of Chicago / Art Resource: p. 112; Art Resource: pp. 1, 8, 10 BL, 10 BR, 12 B (Borromeo), 17 BL, 22 B (Moldvay), 26, 71 BR (Hubert Josse), 32 TL (Manu Sassoonian), 58 T (Saskia), 70, 72 T, 80 B, 86, 93 T (Howard Jensen); © Candida and Rebecca Smith, 1983 / Archives of American Art, Smithsonian Institution / Art Resource: p. 101 TL; The Corcoran Gallery of Art / Art Resource: p. 75 BL; Editorial Photographic Service / Art Resource: pp. 16 T, 24 B, 91 TR, 95 TR; Giraudon / Art Resource: pp. 10 T, 13 TR, 14 B, 15 BR, 21 BR, 31 TL, 36 T, 66, 72 B, 80 T, 100 M; Hirshhorn Museum and Sculpture Garden / Scala / Art Resource: pp. 87 TL, 99 TR, 100 T, 101 TR, 102 T; Isabella Stewart Gardner Museum / Art Resource: p. 82 B; The Jefferson Medical College of Thomas Jefferson University / Art Resource: p. 89 TR; Kunsthistorisches Museum, Vienna / Art Resource: pp. 49 TR, 59; The Metropolitan Museum of Art: pp. 36 B (Rogers Fund, 1933), 48 (Purchase, 1924, Joseph Pulitzer Bequest), 55 (The Cloisters Collection), 62 (Bequest of Benjamin Altman, 1913), 79 (Morris K. Jesup Fund, 1933); The Morgan Library / Art Resource: p. 31 R; Musée de l'Homme, Paris / Art Resource: p. 16 B; Musées Nationaux Paris / Art Resource: pp. 6 T, 21 TL; Museum of Fine Arts, Boston: pp. 74, 81 TL; The Museum of Modern Art: pp. 7 TR (Given anonymously), 7 B and 94 (Acquired through the Lillie P. Bliss Bequest), 103 BL (Purchase); National Audubon Society with the Cooperation of the National Gallery of Art, Washington, D.C.: p. 78 B; National Gallery of Art, Washington, D.C. / Art Resource: pp. 71 BL, 89 B, 96, 107; Naturhistorisches Museum, Vienna / Art Resource: p. 6 B; New York Public Library / Art Resource: p. 78 T; The Pennsylvania Western Conservancy / Art Resource: p. 84; The Philadelphia Museum of Art / Art Resource: pp. 75 R (The George W. Elkins Collection), 92 (The Louise and Walter Arensberg Collection); Praeger Graz: p. 7 TL; Scala / Art Resource: pp. 4, 11 L, 12 T, 13 TL, 13 BL, 13 BR, 14 T, 15 T, 15 BL, 17 R, 18, 20 TL, 20 BL, 20 R, 21 TR, 21 BL, 22 TR, 22 TL, 23 T, 23 BL, 23 BR, 24 T, 25 R, 25 BL, 28, 29 TL, 29 BL, 29 R, 32 B, 33 T, 33 B, 34, 37, 38, 40 T, 40 B, 41 B, 42, 44 T, 44 B, 45, 46 T, 46 B, 47, 49 TL, 49 BL, 50 T, 50 B, 51, 52, 53 T, 53 BL, 53 BR, 54, 56 T, 56 B, 57, 58 B, 60 T, 60 B, 61, 63 T, 63 B, 64, 65 TL, 65 TR, 65 BL, 68, 69, 71 T, 73 B, 76, 77 T, 77 B, 81 TR, 81 B, 82 T, 83, 87 TR, 87 B, 88, 89 TL (Joseph Martin), 90, 91 TL, 91 B, 95 TL, 95 B, 97 T, 97 BL, 97 BR, 98 T, 99 TL, 99 BL, 100 B, 103 T, 108, 110; Sotheby Parke-Bernet / Art Resource: pp. 2, 17 TL, 75 TL, 93 B, 98 B, 99 BR, 101 BL, 101 BR, 102 B, 103 BR, 104 TL, 104 TR, 104 B, 105 TL, 105 TR, 105 BL, 105 BR, 106; Trinity Library, Dublin / Art Resource: p. 30; University Museum of National Antiquities, Oslo / Art Resource: p. 31 BL; The University Museum, University of Pennsylvania / Art Resource: p. 11 R.

BOOK DESIGN: *Jos. Trautwein/Bentwood Studio*

Library of Congress Cataloging in Publication Data:
Davidson, Marshall B.
A history of art.
Includes index.
1. Art—History. I. Title.
N5300.D27   1984   709   83-16110
ISBN: 0-394-85181-1 (pbk.); 0-394-95181-6 (lib. bdg.)

Manufactured in the United States of America
1 2 3 4 5 6 7 8 9 0

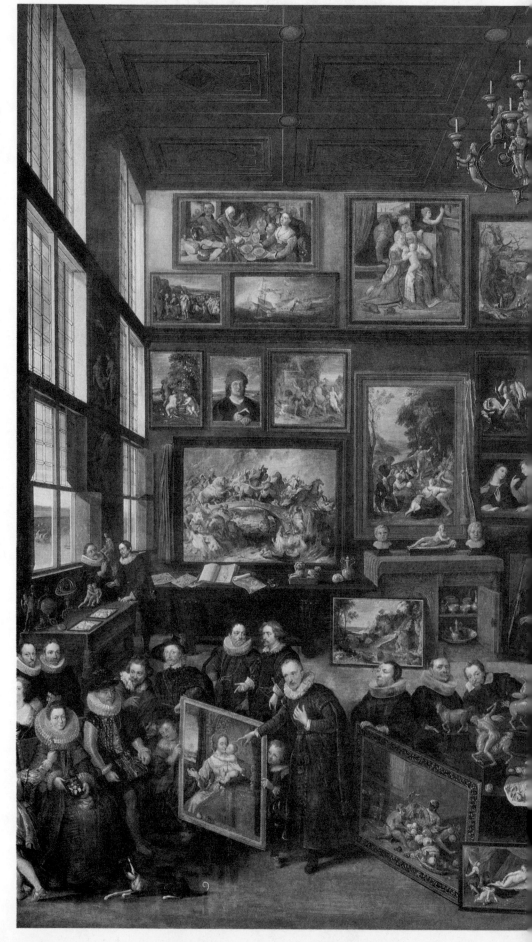

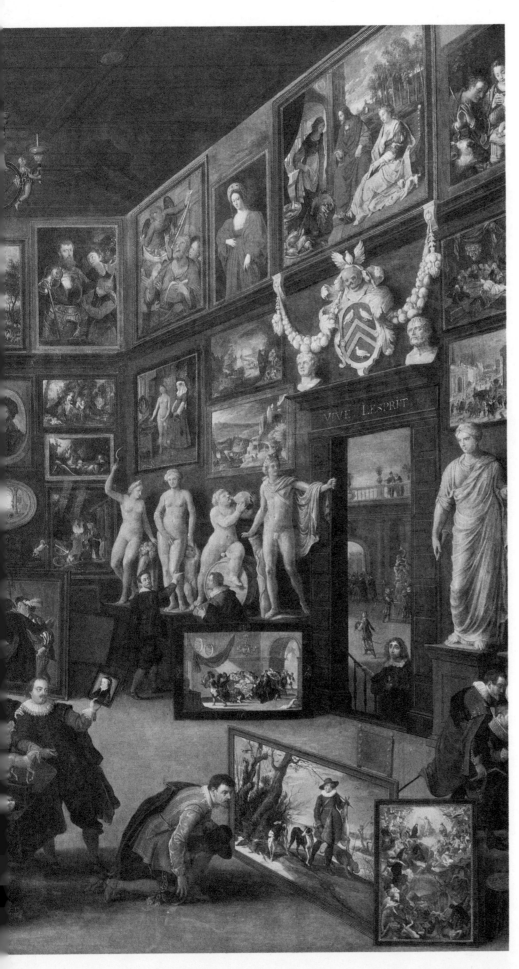

CONTENTS

Willem van Haecht II, *The Art Studio
of Cornelius van der Geest*, 1628

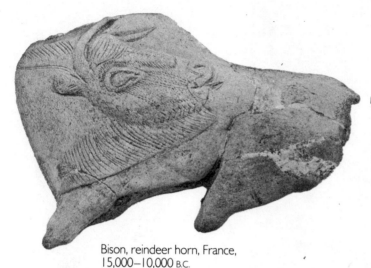

Bison, reindeer horn, France,
15,000–10,000 B.C.

THE
BEGINNINGS
OF ART

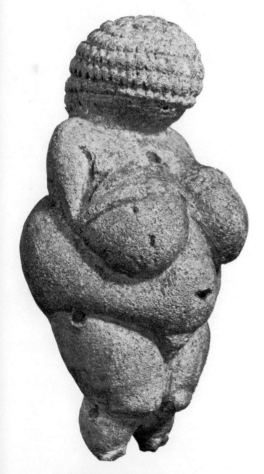

Venus of Willendorf, stone,
Austria, 25,000–20,000 B.C.

Man drew and painted and sculpted figures long before he could read or write, before he learned how to grow his own food, and probably before he knew how to build a permanent shelter to protect him from the weather. No one can say just when the earliest artists began to create. But it was surely before the dawn of recorded history—about the time the fourth and most recent Ice Age was ending. That was between 12,000 and 25,000 years ago.

That great span of years—many times longer than the time that separates our own day from the birth of Christ—is known as the Old Stone Age. It is so called because our very remote ancestors who lived then did not know about metals. With tools made of stone they produced the weapons and other equipment they needed in their primitive lives. These people were cave dwellers who hunted wild beasts and who gathered other food as best they could, but who grew or herded nothing themselves.

Some of these prehistoric people developed skills that enabled them to cover the walls of their dark caves with very lifelike paintings, mostly of the animals they depended on for survival—bison, reindeer, and others. The individuals who created these images were among the first specialists in history. Because of the importance a tribe placed upon their work, such "artists" were probably relieved of other community chores.

Quotation marks were put around the word "artists" in the last sentence to call attention to the fact that neither they nor those who first looked at their paintings considered them works of art. Rather they viewed them as forms of magic. The paintings were seen as actual re-creations of the living animals they so closely resembled. And, it was believed, what man had copied he could also control. If an artist pictured swarms of animals roaming and leaping about, it seemed certain that such game would be plentiful. If he showed the animals pierced by a spear or an arrow, he believed that his tribe's hunting would be successful and its food supply replenished. These Stone Age hunters had no horses. To run down their prey through a bleak and hostile wilderness, to slay huge and powerful beasts with only the crudest weapons, they needed all the help they could hope for. The cave paintings, it was thought, enlisted the help of the spirits.

6

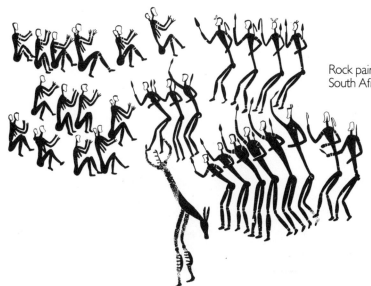

Rock painting of a Bushman dance,
South Africa, 4000 B.C.

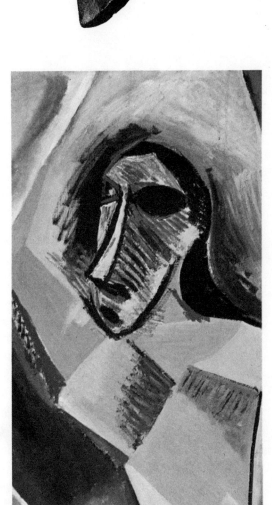

Itumba mask, wood,
Gabon/Zaire, Africa

How such remarkably lifelike images could possibly have been produced in the black depths of underground caves remains a mystery. The artists took advantage of the rough contours of the stone walls to give their paintings a third dimension, almost as if they were modeled in the round. To add to a sense of reality, the animals were given their natural colors with pigments made of different earths, charcoal, and the like. A great many thousands of years ago, when the paintings were first seen in flickering torchlight (which added a suggestion of movement), it must have seemed like a magical performance.

Both animal and human figures were also carved in animal horn, stone, and other durable materials. They, too, were supposed to have magical qualities, and they had the advantage of being portable. The famous *Venus of Willendorf* is not conventionally beautiful. Instead her broad hips and large breasts represent a female ideally shaped for childbearing and nursing. She might have been called on in a fertility ritual for an increase in a clan or tribe, thus ensuring its survival in a world of dangers.

Down to our own day, primitive peoples in different parts of the world have used painted and carved images to secure their well-being on earth or in some life hereafter. Only recently have these been considered works of art, apart from their original purpose. We can find in them evidence of very old cultures, different from ours but with a rich heritage from the past. Seen from this angle, they have had some influence on modern art. For example, a face painted by Picasso early in this century shows a marked resemblance to a wooden mask fashioned by some unknown African tribesman of the past.

Before the end of the Stone Age, some pictures were composed of simple stick figures showing people in action. They resemble signs, rather than realistic images, and often appear in storytelling patterns. Before letters and alphabets were invented, these abstract symbols were used in place of writing. From all this we may assume that art, religion, and writing had their beginnings in magical practices.

With the ending of the last Ice Age the face of Europe changed. The bleak tundras gave way to forests and other vegetation. Different animals moved into this new habitat. The scene was set for fresh adventures by humankind.

Pablo Picasso, *Les Demoiselles d'Avignon* (detail),
1906–1907

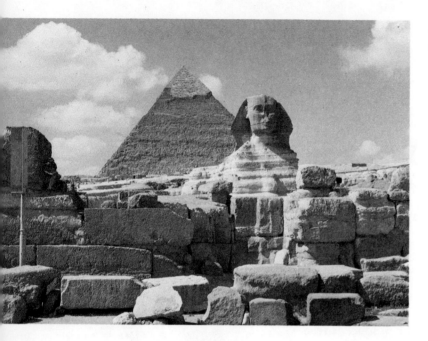

ANCIENT ART

About three or four thousand years B.C., in a few favored parts of the world, man emerged from the Old Stone Age into the New Stone Age. He learned to use such metals as bronze and copper. Growing food and breeding domestic animals came into common use. During this time people moved out of caves into shelters they made for themselves. They began to live in larger communities, which grew into cities. Most important, they learned how to read and write. In short, they became civilized.

Now they could keep records and exchange ideas and information with others, even over a distance. They could learn from one another and could develop new outlooks on life. By using new materials and techniques, they could express those outlooks in art forms the cavemen could not have imagined.

Two of the earliest civilizations where all this came about appeared at around the same time (about 3500 B.C.): one

in Egypt along the banks of the Nile River, the other in Mesopotamia ("the land between the rivers") in the valley watered by the Tigris and Euphrates rivers in what is now Iraq.

Protected by surrounding deserts and, to a degree, by the Mediterranean Sea, the Egyptians were rarely disturbed by invaders. Their prosperity was also ensured by the fruitfulness of their land. Each year the Nile, swollen by spring rains in the southern highlands, flooded its banks and the broad plains of its delta and left an annual deposit of rich, fertile soil. To this natural phenomenon, which assured an annual harvest of life-sustaining crops, ancient Egypt owed not only its wealth but its very existence. In this relative isolation Egyptian civilization and arts showed little change for more than three thousand years. It was one of the earliest and most long-lived civilizations in history.

Most of the finest Egyptian art comes from the tombs of royal families. Life after death, the Egyptians believed, would be a continuation of life on earth with all its pleasures and privileges—at least for the wellborn. The bodies of the dead were preserved as mummies so that their souls would have a place to live. Tombs were decorated with likenesses of the dead and their treasures, and with scenes of daily life as they had enjoyed it. The largest of these tombs were the great pyramids, one of which was made of more than two million stone blocks, each weighing more than two and a half tons. The labor and engineering required by such stupendous operations is difficult to imagine.

In spite of the pyramid builders' precautions to protect their remains and their treasures from violation, almost all of the royal tombs were robbed over the years. Some idea of what the pyramids may have originally contained was given when the untouched tomb of Tutankhamen was discovered in 1922 to the amazement of the world. He was just a minor pharaoh who died when he was still a teenager. Yet his relatively small tomb brimmed with incalculably rich works of art.

The Egyptians believed that the spirit of their gods resided in certain birds and animals, such as the hawk and the cat, whose images they worshiped. Since the Egyptian ruler, or pharaoh, was considered godlike, he is often shown in the form of an animal or with some animal features. As a sphinx, for instance, he has the body of a lion and a human head.

During this period Mesopotamia was occupied by one ruling group after another—the Sumerians, the Babylonians, the Assyrians, and the Persians. The region became a melting pot of different peoples. Each of these passed on to the others its traditions and its religious beliefs, as well as its practical skills and useful knowledge. In this flat land, shrines were built atop man-made mountains called ziggurats. (The biblical tower of Babel was one of these.)

On these shrines were placed offerings to the gods, who were identified with the forces that controlled the universe—the moon and the stars, the floodwaters, and so on. In those shrines were also placed images of the priests and rulers who, as agents of the gods, could ask them for mercy and favor.

Far back in time, the Sumerians wrote down accounts of how they believed their river-bound world had been created. The stories they recorded are echoed in passages from Genesis in the Old Testament, for ancient Hebrew writers were almost certainly familiar with them when they related their stories of the Garden of Eden, the Flood, and other biblical tales. It was also in Mesopotamia that the world's first legal codes were drawn up.

Between two and three thousand years B.C., other peoples settled in the eastern Mediterranean: some were known as the Minoans, who lived on the island of Crete; others we call the Mycenaeans, who inhabited the nearby Greek mainland. The Minoans and the Mycenaeans developed civilizations equal in importance to those of Egypt and Mesopotamia, but quite different in their arts and customs.

Both were seafaring people, fishermen, traders, and pirates. The more peaceable Minoans lived in unfortified settlements. The ruling classes built handsome palaces and private villas whose walls were covered with colorful paintings and whose comforts included bathrooms. They built no temples. But in sacred places they worshiped a mother goddess and to her sacrificed bulls, probably with a double axe. The horns of a bull and the double axe were cult symbols that often marked those shrines.

The more warlike Mycenaeans protected their cities with massive stone walls. In time the Mycenaeans conquered the Minoans and absorbed much of their culture. Then, around 1100 B.C., disaster came to these lands in the form of earthquakes, fires, and invasion by other peoples from the north, and these first European civilizations were no more. Memories of their ancient glory, however, would be forever recalled in the epic poems of Homer.

Some fifteen hundred years before Columbus discovered the New World, another totally different but advanced civilization had taken root and would soon flower in the rain forests of Central America. These people, the Maya Indians, had a developed system of writing, a refined form of architecture, and a special genius for mathematics and astronomy. In their jungle world, without knowledge of metal tools, wheeled vehicles, or beasts of burden, they built large ceremonial areas. Here they erected towering temples, like the ziggurats, amid fields they had cleared to raise maize, or corn.

Most Mayan art, like that of the earlier civilizations already mentioned, represents the gods who controlled the rain, the sun, the wind, the water, the growth of maize, and the rites performed in their worship. As their unique civilization declined, other Indian peoples rose to importance—notably the Aztecs of Mexico and the Incas of Peru. In the 16th century the Spanish conquistadores (conquerors), mounted on horses and equipped with cannons, both new and terrifying to the Indians, took over their lands and the control of their lives.

Sumer was one of the oldest countries in Mesopotamia, which is now Iraq. It was made up of various city-states that often warred with one another for supremacy, and against foreign invaders. The mosaic panel reproduced here, known as the *Peace Standard* of Ur—one of the principal city-states of Sumer—pictures a feast celebrating a victory. In the top row, a ruler sits facing his officers. At the right, a female dancer or singer is accompanied by a musician playing a harp framed with a bull's head. In the middle row, various animals and fish are being taken to the banquet scene. At the bottom, captured beasts and porters carry booty won in battle.

The *Billygoat and Tree* is a strong and colorful image of the natural world, which the Sumerians believed was ruled by supernatural forces. These spirits often took the shape of strange and powerful beasts such as this remarkable goat.
    The tree is covered with gold leaf, as are parts of the goat. The base is inlaid with lapis lazuli and shells.

The Assyrians destroyed and rebuilt Babylon (see below). Its luxury then became legendary under King Nebuchadnezzar. The so-called Hanging Gardens were one of the Seven Wonders of the World. The city's walls were decorated with colorfully **glazed brick** on which enormous reliefs of lions fiercely glowered down at visitors.

This lifelike **praying figure,** its hands and face covered with gold leaf, may represent Hammurabi, the great king who founded the Babylonian empire in Mesopotamia about 1792 B.C. The code of laws by which he ruled his land, the first known legal code, is one of the most important documents of ancient history.

The Assyrians were a powerful people whose profession was war. Their mighty king, **Ashurbanipal,** is pictured here in a stone relief slaying a lion.

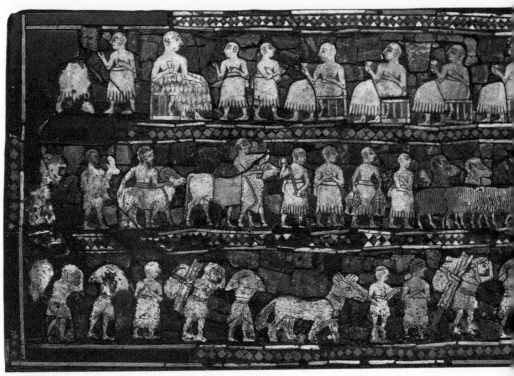

Peace Standard, Ur, Mesopotamia, about 2600 B.C.

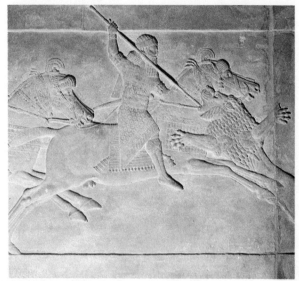

King Ashurbanipal Hunting a Lion, stone, Assyria, 7th century B.C.

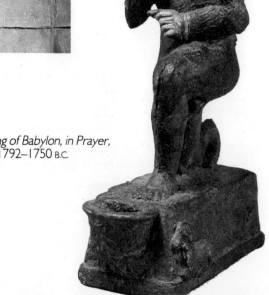

Hammurabi (?), King of Babylon, in Prayer, terra cotta, about 1792–1750 B.C.

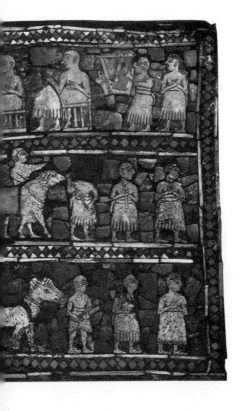

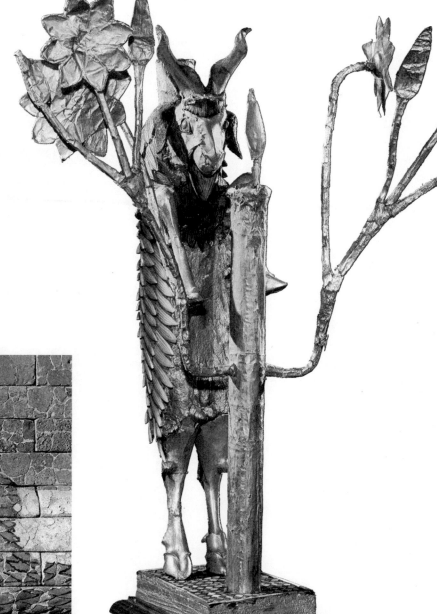

Billygoat and Tree, wood, gold, and lapis lazuli, Ur, Mesopotamia, about 2600 B.C.

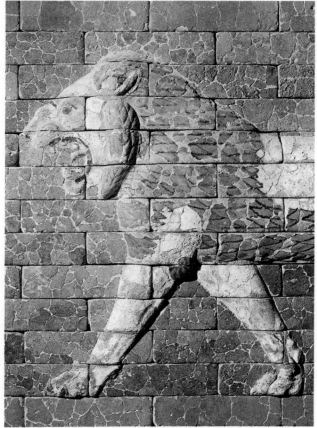

Glazed brick panel (detail), Babylon, 6th century B.C.

11

The *Book of the Dead* contains a collection of magical spells intended to guide the soul of a dead person safely through the realm of the gods. These papyrus scrolls include pictures of animal-headed gods with scales on which they weighed the heart of a deceased person against a feather, the symbol of truth. If the scales balanced, the dead one's spirit could enter the hereafter without fear.

The Egyptians imagined that supernatural beetles, or **scarabs,** pushed the sun across the sky, the way a dung beetle on earth pushes its egg in front of it. The scarab in this piece of jewelry from Tutankhamen's tomb was believed to protect the dead pharaoh with its magical properties.

Many Egyptian tombs contained small figures of **hippopotamuses** placidly standing with designs of lotus and other flora of their native marshland habitat painted on their bodies. These animals were associated with one of the goddesses who influenced the lives of mortals and who commanded respect.

Among the wealth of other treasures discovered in Tutankhamen's tomb was this **gold inner coffin,** inlaid with enamel and semiprecious stones. Tutankhamen holds in his arms a crook and a flail, symbols of his royal authority.

One of the most memorable portraits from ancient Egypt is this sculpture of **Queen Nefertiti,** bejeweled and wearing an ornate headdress.

The walls of **royal tombs**—like the tomb of the beautiful Queen Nefertiti—were covered with paintings of pharaohs and their queens along with the strange, partly animal gods whose supernatural powers they claimed to share. Note that the pharaoh is portrayed with an animal god's head.

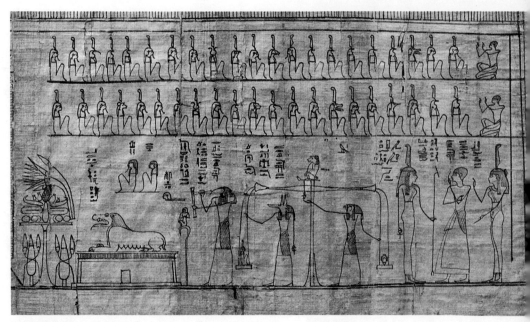

Book of the Dead (detail), Egypt, about 7th century B.C.

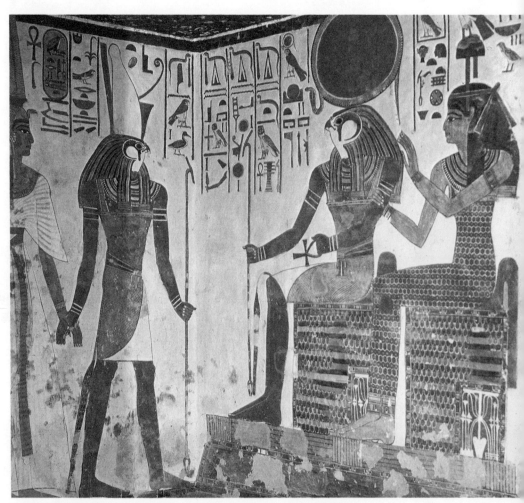

Fresco from the Tomb of Nefertiti (detail), Egypt, about 14th century B.C.

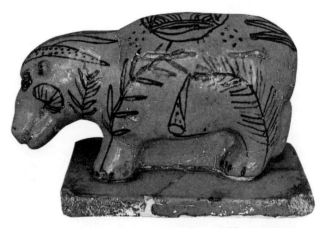

Hippopotamus, faience, Egypt, 14th century B.C.

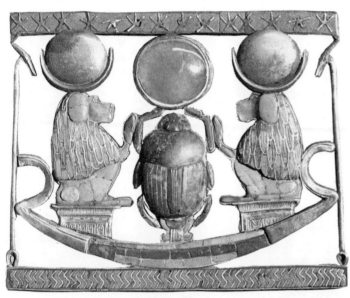

Scarab from the Tomb of King Tutankhamen, Egypt, 1340 B.C.

King Tutankhamen coffin cover
(detail), gold with
semiprecious stones, Egypt, 1340 B.C.

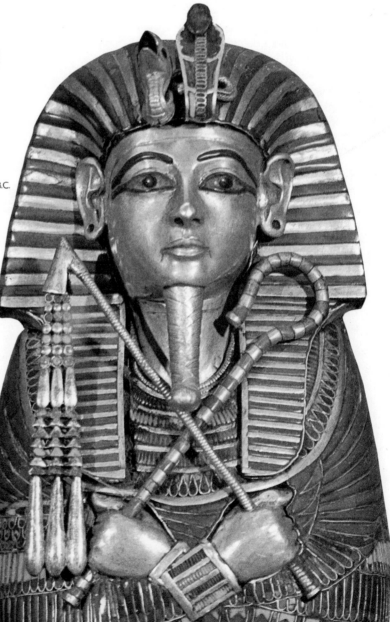

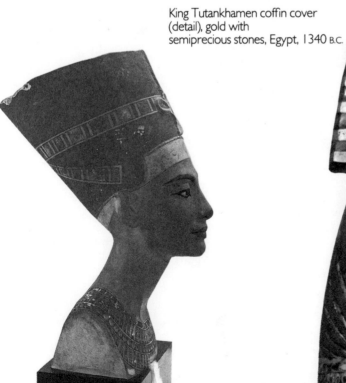

Queen Nefertiti, painted limestone,
Egypt, about 1360 B.C.

A **gold mask** was placed over the face of a Mycenaean ruler upon his death. When this one was discovered, it was believed to have belonged to Agamemnon. According to ancient Greek mythology, he was the leader of the Greek forces in the Trojan War. Agamemnon was called by Homer in the *Iliad* "the king of men." His city was the richest and most powerful of all the early Greek city-states.

Bull leaping was a favorite sport among the Minoans (residents of ancient Crete), practiced by youths of both sexes. As illustrated in this **wall painting** from the palace at Knossos, an acrobat would grasp the horns of a bull. When the beast tossed his head in anger, the athlete would fly into the air and somersault over the bull's back. A girl standing behind the bull is waiting to steady the jumper as he lands on the ground.

Images of writhing octopuses were often used in the art of people living along the Aegean Sea—as on this **pitcher**, or *amphora*. Such figures recall how dependent these people were on the seas that surrounded them.

A wall made of massive stone blocks surrounded the city of Mycenae, where the great heroes celebrated by Homer flourished. The wall is pierced by the **Lion Gate**, so called because of the figures of two lionesses placed above it to guard the entrance. It is the oldest surviving example of monumental sculpture in Greece.

Women played an important role in the religious ceremonies of the Minoans. The **ceramic statue** shown here may represent one of the female deities who were worshiped in sacred groves. She is outfitted in a long flounced skirt, has an elaborate hairdo and exposed breasts, and in each of her upraised hands she holds a snake.

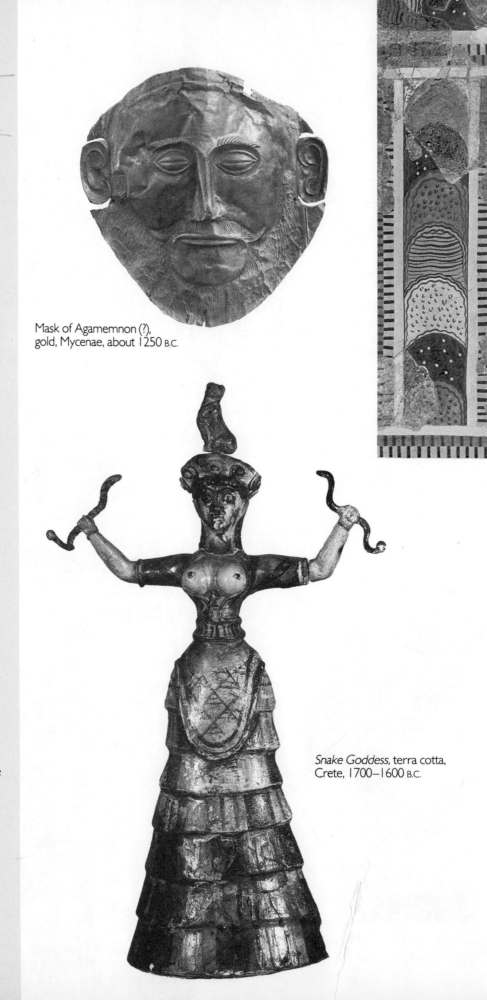

Mask of Agamemnon (?), gold, Mycenae, about 1250 B.C.

Snake Goddess, terra cotta, Crete, 1700–1600 B.C.

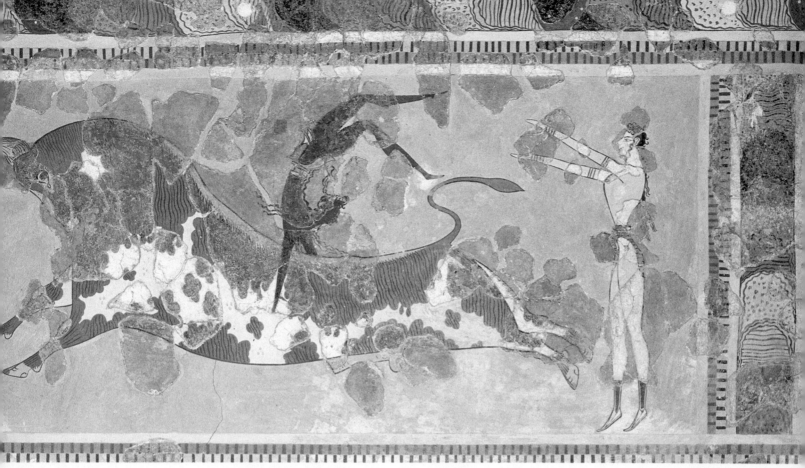
Bull-leaping fresco, Crete, about 1500 B.C.

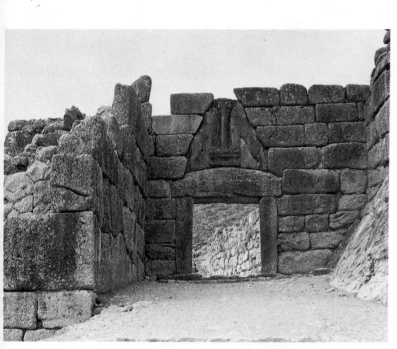
Lion Gate, Mycenae, about 1250 B.C.

Octopus pitcher, Crete, about 1500 B.C.

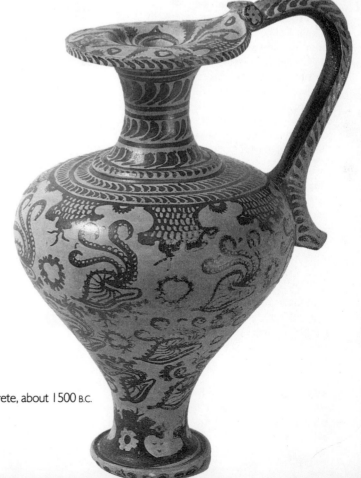

15

Long before the Spanish Conquest in the New World, the Mayan culture had almost disappeared. Evidence of Mayan accomplishments had been covered over by the dense tropical jungles. One of the most impressive demonstrations of Mayan art is a series of **wall paintings** representing a battle and its aftermath. These vivid scenes were painted in a small temple about A.D. 800, the year Charlemagne was crowned emperor in distant Rome. They remained hidden in the jungle until 1946 when natives led archaeologists to the site, which became known as Bonampak ("painted walls").

In the course of their religious and other ceremonies, the Mayans burned quantities of incense. A great number of **incense burners** have survived. Many of them take the form of one or another of the Mayan gods. Reproduced here is the lid of one incense burner, which shows the butterfly god in a canoe, with flattened, outspread wings and a large, unusual headdress.

Maize, or corn, was the basis of ancient Mayan life. It was served and eaten at every meal. Every stage of the crop's growth was marked with religious rituals. The Mayan's cornfield was said to be more dear to him than his family. It was believed that the gods had created man himself from this precious grain. The **corn god** was the most revered of the Mayan deities, and statues of him—such as this one modeled in terra cotta—were placed in tombs and temples.

As the Mayan culture declined, other Indian peoples—such as the Incas in Peru and the Aztecs in Mexico—developed wealth, power, and distinctive art forms. These peoples remained untouched by European influences until the Spanish conquerors overran their lands in the 16th century. A **gold statuette** of a woman reminds us that Peru was the birthplace of American metallurgy. It was the first nation in this hemisphere to separate gold, silver, and copper from ore.

This enameled wooden **head of a puma** was also made in Peru, probably after the Spanish Conquest. It served as a vase.

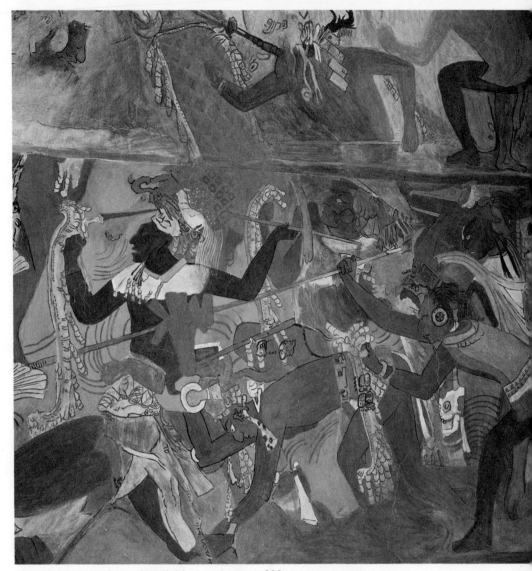

Mayan battle scene fresco (detail), Mexico, about A.D. 800

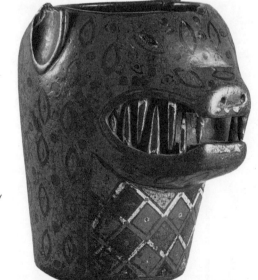

Head of a puma, wood, Peru, about 16th century

16

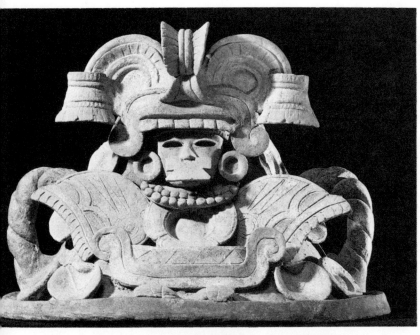

Lid of incense burner, terra cotta, Mexico, about A.D. 250–650

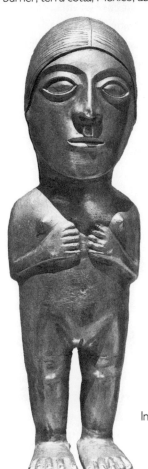

Mayan corn god, terra cotta,
Mexico, A.D. 692

Inca statuette, gold, Peru, 1438–1532

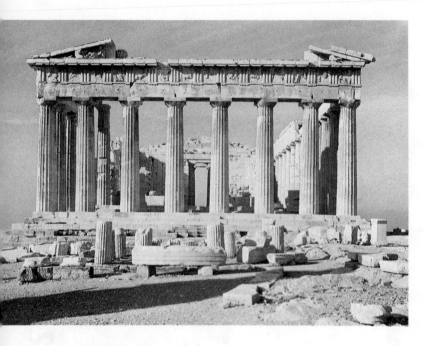

CLASSICAL ART

The period of Greek history from 800 B.C. to 600 B.C. is called a "dark age." One of the few things known is that the land was invaded by people from the north called Dorians. Then, about 600 B.C., a new era dawned. This marked the true birth of western civilization and western art. People began to believe in reason rather than in magic. Instead of worshiping animal gods, these Greeks created gods in their own image. Their gods had all the traits of humankind, both good and bad. They could be understood in human terms.

Temples built to honor Greek gods and goddesses could just as easily have been made to house men and women. Nothing like these very orderly, serene structures of gleaming white marble with vividly colored details had ever been seen before. The best known example is the Parthenon, a temple sacred to the goddess Athena that stands on the Acropolis, a hill overlooking Athens, Greece. Everywhere the Greeks colonized, from Sicily in the west to Asia Minor

in the east, they built similar buildings. Future societies would regard them as models of architectural perfection.

Greek statues and paintings of gods differed little from those of mortal beings. Unlike the ancient Egyptians, the classical Greeks were less interested in the dead than in the living. Artists studied the anatomy of the human body. They were the first to understand how muscles and bones controlled every change in the position of the body. As a result, for the first time in history artists created sculptures of men and women, at ease or in action, that seemed almost as natural as living beings. Perfect living beings, it should be added, for the Greeks had in mind figures with ideal proportions.

The human body was honored in sports as well as in art. Nude male athletes competed at the Olympic Games. These were held every four years in honor of the gods and were immensely popular. Victorious athletes were celebrated in poetry, sculpture, and painting.

Greek painters were as famed as the architects and sculptors, but their greatest works have been destroyed. We can form some idea of what Greek paintings may have been like from the figures and scenes painted on pottery. Happily these have survived in great numbers. They show myths of gods and heroes as well as the Greeks at war, at worship, at work, at play, and at home. Such pottery was exported all around the Mediterranean world and beyond. It remains a pictorial library of Greek thought and life.

Greek culture reached a height in Athens under the leadership of the great statesman Pericles in the 5th century B.C. It was then that the Parthenon was built. At Marathon and other sites the Greeks, although greatly outnumbered, had recently won great victories over invading forces from Persia, victories that were among the most decisive events in the history of the West. The Parthenon was raised in tribute to Athena for those victories.

As Greece was approaching this most glorious period of its history, other peoples, known to us as the Etruscans, came to power in Italy in areas north of the Greek colonies in that land. No one is certain where they came from. Their language has proved very difficult to decipher. We know the Etruscans best from their art. They were fierce warriors and skilled metalworkers, as their weapons, armor, and jewelry prove.

The Etruscans were an intensely religious people who worshiped a number of different gods. Like the Egyptians, they equipped their tombs with all the things the dead might need in the afterlife. There they also placed images of the dead, who were frequently shown as a man and woman reclining on a couch, as if attending a banquet. The walls of tombs were painted with scenes of daily life. From these we learn, among other things, that music and dance were important Etruscan pastimes.

In many of their rituals and beliefs the Etruscans anticipated the Romans who would conquer them. Etruscan rulers wore purple robes as a symbol of office, a custom that the Romans adopted. Etruscans, like the Romans after them, read the future by examining the livers of sheep that had been slaughtered for this purpose. The Etruscans usually laid out their cities on a gridiron plan, which the Romans were to do as well.

Rome was organized as an Etruscan city-state in 753 B.C. on a site, legend tells us, where the abandoned twins Romulus and Remus were suckled by a she-wolf. About 400 B.C. the Etruscan rulers were overthrown and a Roman republic established. The Romans had a genius for government and an urge to conquer. Within a relatively few centuries they had expanded that republic into the largest empire the world has ever known. Roman law and language (Latin) were known and respected from northern Britain to southern Russia.

In their arts the Romans borrowed from all the peoples they had conquered. Most of what we know of Greek sculpture, for example, comes from copies of Greek originals that were manufactured for the Roman market. In Roman sculptured portraits, however, the ideal image of the Greeks was replaced by a realism that showed every wart and sagging muscle.

The Romans also brought their own contributions to conquered lands. Like the Etruscans, they were great civil engineers. Everywhere they went they built remarkable roads, aqueducts (waterways), and public baths. Roman architects were the first to use the arch as a basic element in construction. Imperial Rome was dotted with magnificent triumphal arches, raised to celebrate the victories of its emperors and their armies. Great amphitheaters were built in many parts of Europe to accommodate the crowds that came to witness chariot races, circuses, and gladiator combats. In all their construction the Romans made wide use of concrete; they were the first to do so.

Roman painting is known largely from surviving wall paintings, many of which decorated the interiors of villas and townhouses of the well-to-do. The best known of these can be seen in the ancient cities of Pompeii and Herculaneum, which were quickly covered with ashes when nearby Mount Vesuvius erupted in A.D. 79. By that great tragedy the structures were preserved almost intact for centuries.

Under Roman rule a large part of the western world lived in peace for several hundred years. It was called the Pax Romana, the Roman Peace. Then the great empire started to fall apart. The imperial machinery gradually lost its power to hold together and to serve the great mixture of peoples that had been subdued and brought under its single government.

We can learn a great deal about Greek art and history from the large number of **coins** that were designed by highly skilled specialists. Among other things, they make up a portrait gallery of ancient gods and heroes.

A marble statue of a nude youth, *Kouros*, is one of many similar figures made early in the development of Greek sculpture, before the anatomy of the human body was clearly understood. Such figures were all originally painted with bright colors. So little of the color has survived the years, and we have become so accustomed to seeing Greek sculpture and architecture as pure white creations, that it is hard to imagine how they appeared when they were first finished.

The perky little pottery owl served as a **perfume vase.** It was modeled to fit neatly in the hand of a lady.

Two of the most famous Greek sculptures are the **Nike of Samothrace** (Winged Victory) and the **Venus de Milo.** Both were made late in the classical period and dramatically show how Greek sculptors had by then become capable of making lifelike figures of perfect beauty out of cold marble. Both figures are damaged, but that does not lessen our admiration. The Winged Victory shows the goddess Aphrodite advancing on the prow of a ship into the swirling winds that fill her wings and press her robes tightly against her body.

An early pottery **amphora** (a jar used for carrying wine or oil) is painted with a scene showing the hero Theseus slaying the bull-headed Minotaur, a popular Greek myth. Such painted vessels were highly valued.

A detail of the earliest surviving large bronze statue in Greek art pictures a young **charioteer** and commemorates his victory in the Olympic Games. Originally it stood on a chariot drawn by four horses, which he had driven to his triumph in the games. The pupils of his eyes were made of colored stones; his hair, eyelids, and lips were lightly gilded.

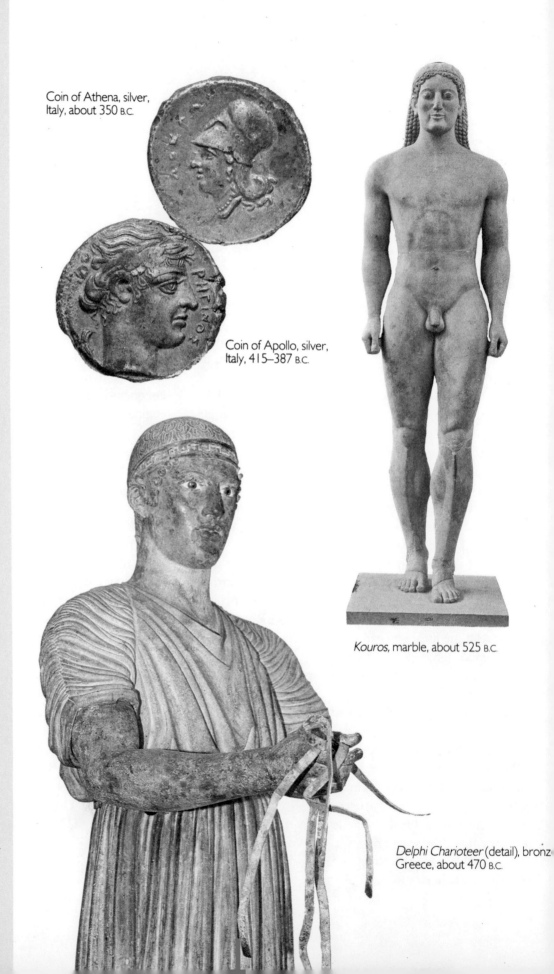

Coin of Athena, silver, Italy, about 350 B.C.

Coin of Apollo, silver, Italy, 415–387 B.C.

Kouros, marble, about 525 B.C.

Delphi Charioteer (detail), bronze Greece, about 470 B.C.

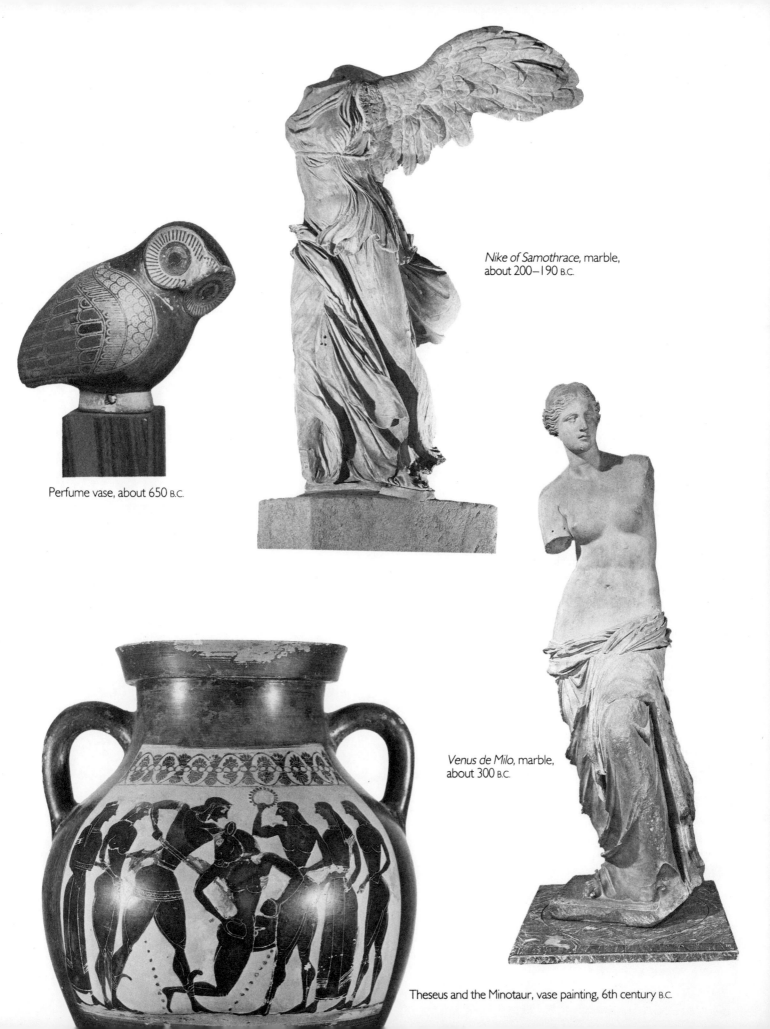

Nike of Samothrace, marble,
about 200–190 B.C.

Perfume vase, about 650 B.C.

Venus de Milo, marble,
about 300 B.C.

Theseus and the Minotaur, vase painting, 6th century B.C.

The back of a **bronze mirror** is engraved with the figure of a soothsayer looking for omens in the liver of a sacrificial animal.

The Etruscans made many **bronze statuettes** of armed warriors ready for battle. In this example a soldier, practically sheathed in bronze with his shield at the ready, is about to hurl a spear.

The walls of Etruscan tombs were painted with colorful scenes of daily life. One of the best known and best preserved of these **frescoes** shows dancing musicians. The central figure plays a double flute, and one of his companions holds a lyre, a stringed instrument. The Etruscans were renowned throughout the ancient world for their love of music.

This detail of a life-size painted terracotta statue of **Apollo** is a masterpiece of Etruscan art. Originally it was one of four figures that stood on the ridge of the roof of a temple at Veii, not far from Rome. It is a very powerful image, more animated and more realistically modeled than Greek sculptures of the same early period.

An Etruscan ceremonial **helmet,** modeled after Greek ones, was designed to protect the warrior's cheeks and nose as well as his head. It is finely decorated with battle scenes.

In this bronze group the abandoned twins **Romulus and Remus** are shown being suckled by a she-wolf. According to Roman legend, when the twins were grown men they founded the city of Rome on the site where they had been discovered by an Etruscan shepherd. The twins were added to the she-wolf statue in the 15th century.

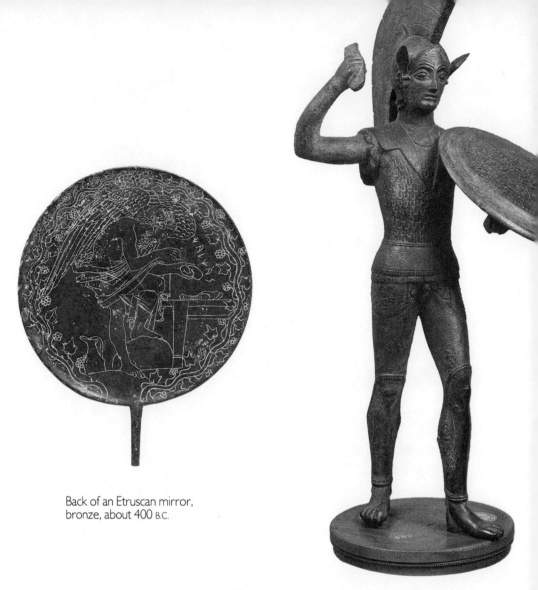

Back of an Etruscan mirror, bronze, about 400 B.C.

Etruscan statuette, bronze, mid-5th century B.C.

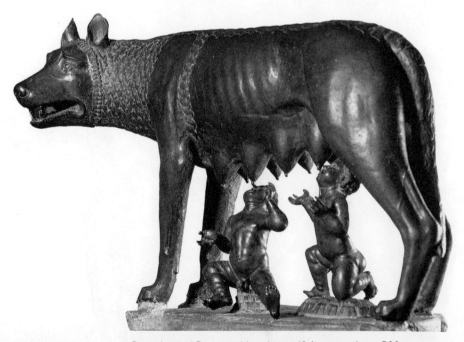

Romulus and Remus with a she-wolf, bronze, about 500 B.C.

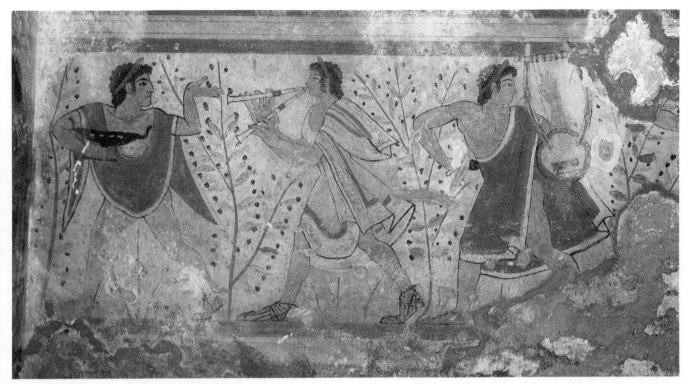

Fresco from the Tomb of the Leopards, 5th century B.C.

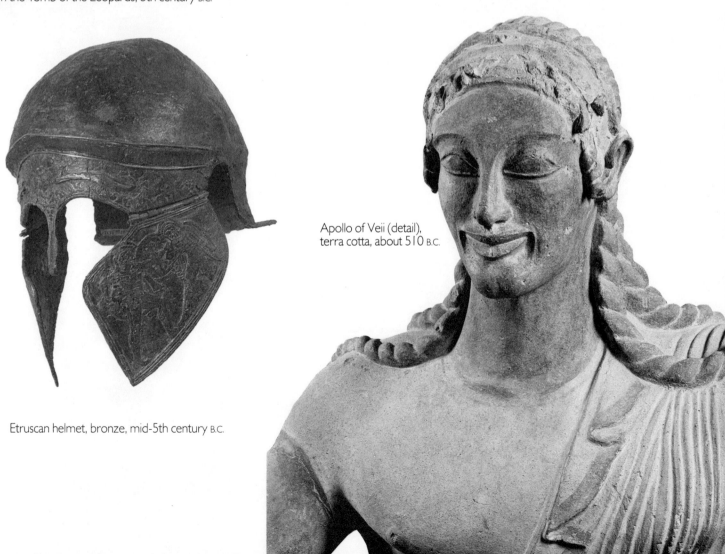

Etruscan helmet, bronze, mid-5th century B.C.

Apollo of Veii (detail),
terra cotta, about 510 B.C.

In much of their art the Romans were strongly influenced by Greek models. An elaborate **floor mosaic,** a portion of which is shown here, depicts the defeat of the Persians under their emperor Darius by the forces of Alexander the Great. It is apparently a copy of an earlier Greek painting.

Shortly before the birth of Christ, the **emperor Augustus** commissioned a larger than life-size statue of himself making a commanding gesture. He and his immediate successors encouraged their subjects to consider them divine rulers. And there appears to be something superhuman in this heroic standing figure.

The Romans were masters of **still-life painting.** A fine example shows a number of peaches with a glass jar half filled with water. The clarity of the glass and water and the roundness of the fruit come remarkably close to re-creating the actual things.

As we can see from the many structures that survive today, the Romans were unsurpassed engineers. With their skillful use of the arch, they could build aqueducts that spanned wide rivers and valleys, such as the **Pont du Gard** at Nîmes in southern France. Although it was strictly functional, it is also a very handsome construction.

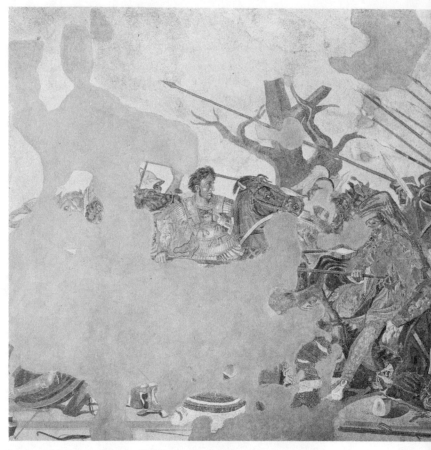

Battle of Alexander and the Persians, mosaic copy of a Greek painting, 1st century B.C.

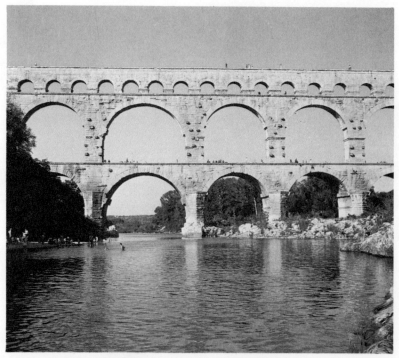

Pont du Gard, France, 1st century B.C.

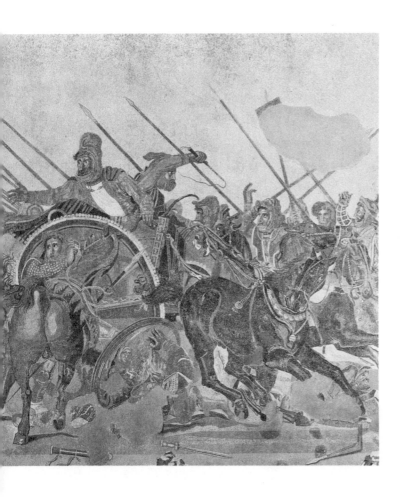

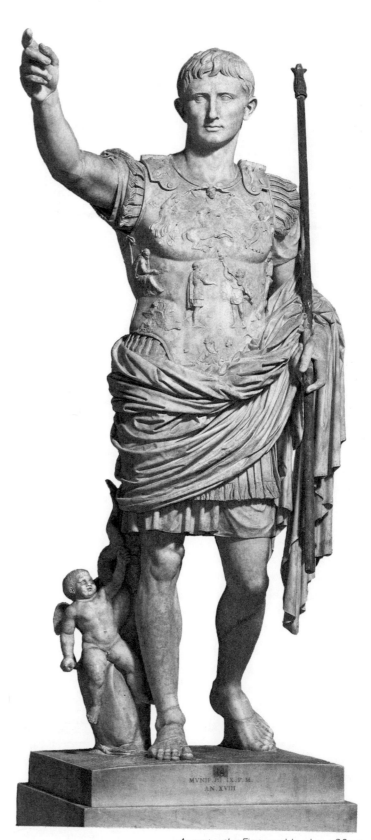

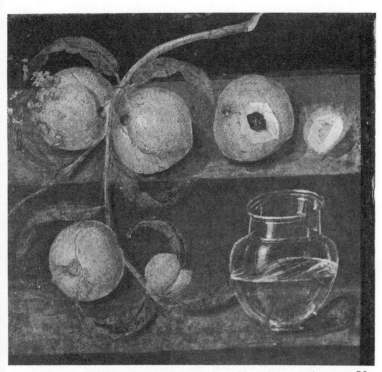

Peaches and Glass Jar, wall painting from Herculaneum, about A.D. 50

Augustus the First, marble, about 20 B.C.

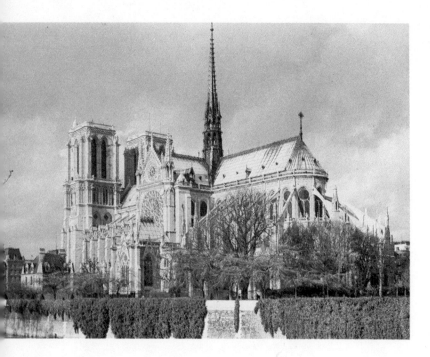

MEDIEVAL ART

The term "Middle Ages" refers to the period in western civilization between ancient and modern times. That was, very roughly, the thousand years between the fall of Rome and the beginning of the Renaissance (from about the 5th to the 15th centuries A.D.). During that long time the arts borrowed from many sources—from ancient Greece and Rome, western Asia, and the tribal cultures of barbarians who invaded Europe as the Roman Empire declined.

The one factor that unifies the long and complex period during which medieval art developed was the authority of the Christian Church. That binding force was felt in law and science, in economics and diplomacy, in literature and art, and even in war. The Church inspired the Crusades—military expeditions of Christians from western Europe to reclaim the Holy Land from the Muslims.

Throughout the Middle Ages most people—ordinary people, that is—could not read. (This was before the invention of the printing press.) The Church used the arts to instruct and uplift its members. The great cathedral of

Chartres in France, for example, was built during this time. It is a great religious encyclopedia made up of no less than 8,000 images in sculpture and stained glass, all teaching the lessons of Christianity.

The earliest Christians were a persecuted sect in the Roman world. Then, in A.D. 313, the emperor Constantine was converted to this new faith. He moved his court from Rome to the ancient fortified town of Byzantium (the city was renamed Constantinople and is now called Istanbul, Turkey). Here, in the eastern capital of the sprawling Roman Empire, was developed the Byzantine style of art in which the Church found its first distinctive expression. In this style human figures and other natural forms are flattened out into what are almost abstract patterns. Divine and saintly subjects seem frozen in rigid poses. Their staring eyes look at us as though from another world—from the very heavens. The emperor and empress were portrayed in the same manner.

This was not altogether surprising, for the eastern rulers thought of themselves as leaders of the Church and, as such, close to divinity. This retreat from the naturalism of Roman art was an important turning point in the history of art. The Byzantine style had its most impressive expression in the glittering mosaics of Hagia Sophia (the Church of Holy Wisdom in Constantinople) and of churches in Ravenna and Venice, Italy, where Byzantine influence remained strong.

While the Roman court at Constantinople held sway with almost oriental splendor in the eastern half of the empire, the court at Rome was losing its authority in the western half. Under Roman rule most of Europe had enjoyed peace for several hundred years. But gradually the imperial machinery lost control of the great mixture of peoples that had been brought together under a single government in that large area. Finally that machinery broke down altogether, and barbarian tribes surged at will across the old frontiers of the empire and spread out over the continent.

These invasions were not so much a cause of Rome's declining power as they were a symptom of it. The invaders came not to destroy Roman civilization but to enjoy its benefits. However, under the weight of their numbers, Roman civilization collapsed. These nomads had an art of their own. It consisted largely of designs that ornamented their weapons, jewelry, and other portable possessions. In full dress, an armed and bejeweled chieftain made an impressive spectacle.

Some semblance of order and unity was slowly restored to Europe with the advance of Christianity. The conversion of the barbarians was mostly the work of medieval monks. In their monasteries they preserved as much of the learning of the past as they could find. The manuscripts they so painstakingly copied by hand were works of art themselves, illuminated with intricate designs that recall those used in barbarian ornament. In either art human figures seldom appear. When they do, they are less important than the surrounding decorative patterns.

Although the invading nomads from the north overran almost all of Europe, and although almost all traces of Roman rule had vanished, the conviction that the Roman Empire still existed in Europe faded very slowly.

In A.D. 800 the French king Charlemagne was crowned the first Holy Roman Emperor by the pope in Rome, who needed his protection against forces that threatened the authority of the Church. But Charlemagne returned to his homeland to administer his huge empire, in which he hoped the glory and the grandeur of the classical past might be revived in a Christian state. In his effort to accomplish this, he brought to his northern court scholars and artists from all over his empire—and beyond. To guide the artists and craftsmen in their work, Charlemagne imported many manuscripts and works of art from the ancient world.

Charlemagne's efforts were interrupted by fresh invasions of Europe. Years before his reign, Moors had crossed over from Africa to occupy Spain. Charlemagne suffered a major defeat when he attempted to drive them out of that land. In his old age he saw the dreaded longboats of the Vikings with their high dragon prows slipping into his realm along the waterways, bringing destruction with them. But once these and other disturbances ended, Europe entered a period of great achievements.

It was in these late medieval years that wonderfully skilled metalworkers hammered out suits of armor for knights to wear in mortal combat or in jousting tournaments. These steel-plated trappings were things of beauty that were, as well, perfectly designed to protect the wearer from head to toe. Other craftsworkers wove the brilliantly colored tapestries that hung in castles and churches to help ward off the wintry chill of bare stone walls. And it was at this time, too, that talented artists painted the exquisite miniatures that illuminated the pages of religious books.

The most complete and magnificent expression of the medieval spirit was incorporated in the Gothic cathedral—essentially a French creation. From France this style of architecture spread rapidly throughout much of Europe. History had rarely seen such a burst of creative activity as Europe witnessed during the 12th, 13th, and 14th centuries, while these great structures were rising everywhere. In the hundred years between 1175 and 1275 eighty cathedrals and nearly 500 other large churches were built in France alone. It was as though magical stone seeds had been sown across the land and left to flower in great webs of masonry. The huge structures were decorated with sculptured images, stained glass windows, and spires that shot up toward the heavens, rising higher than any structures ever before imagined.

The Middle Ages was not simply a middle period in history between classical and modern times. It was a time when the artistic talents of a wide variety of people were forged into shared creations. In this way great contributions were made to art, literature, and human institutions. These contributions provided the means for Renaissance man to find new directions in the endless search for wisdom, truth, and beauty.

The Byzantine style spread to Italy, throughout the Balkans, and to Russia. A mosaic portrait of the eastern Roman **emperor Justinian,** made for the Church of San Vitale in Ravenna, Italy, is a glittering example: The faithful imitation of life that had developed in Roman art gave way here to flat, two-dimensional forms. Human figures seem to have retreated from the natural world into an unearthly one.

That flat style lingered in 13th-century Italian painting by such artists as **Cimabue,** Duccio, and others. It was called the Greek style. Cimabue's *Madonna Enthroned with Angels* is a clear reflection of Byzantine influence in its stiff, formal patterns and flat gold background. In his lifetime Cimabue was recognized as one of Italy's great painters.

The early Christians often pictured Jesus as the **Good Shepherd** guarding his flock. In sculptures he sometimes appears, as here, as a beardless youth dressed in a toga. He might be taken for a pagan shepherd from a Roman pastoral scene.

It was probably about A.D. 900 that the abbot of a recently founded monastery at Rambona, Italy, had a carved **ivory relief** made in two attached panels (called a diptych). Here are pictured, among other things, the Crucifixion, the Virgin and Child, and the suckling twins Romulus and Remus. The static and rigid figures recall the Byzantine manner, but the artist has tried to give them some expression of feeling and has shown them as separate episodes in one story.

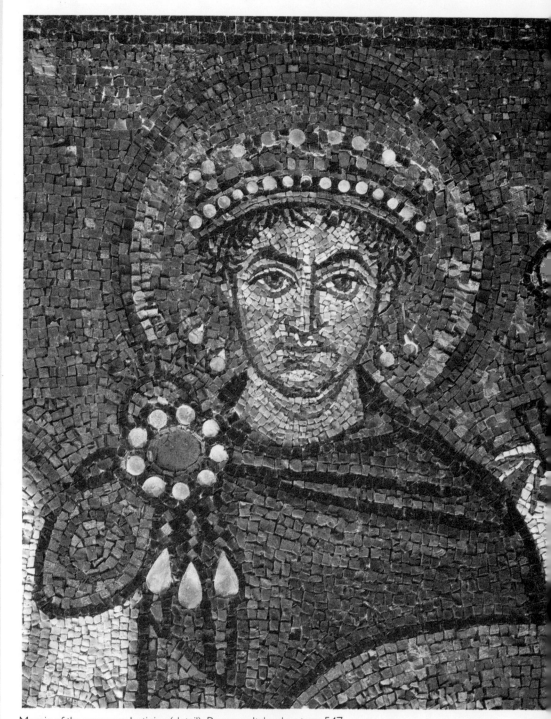

Mosaic of the emperor Justinian (detail), Ravenna, Italy, about A.D. 547

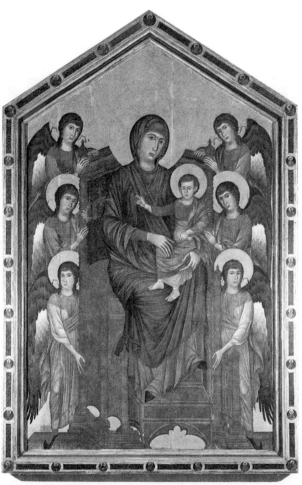

Cimabue, *Madonna Enthroned with Angels,* about 1275

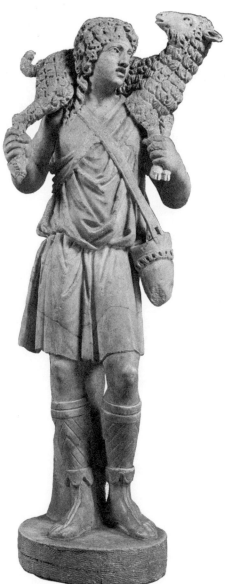

The Good Shepherd, marble,
2nd century A.D.

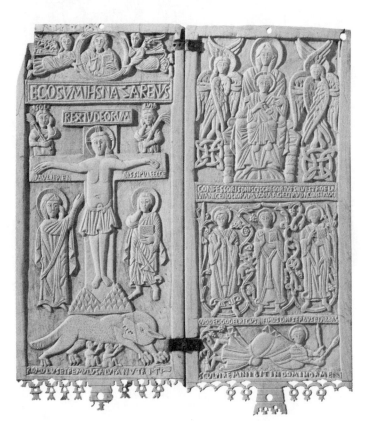

Ivory relief, Rambona, Italy, A.D. 900

Ireland was the first barbarian land to be converted to Christianity. This was begun by Saint Patrick in the 5th century A.D. Within a century the Church there was organized into numerous monasteries where, among their many labors, monks busily copied sacred and scholarly texts. These were handsomely decorated with ornamental designs. One of the most elaborate and beautiful of these is *The Book of Kells*. Boldly illustrated are the Greek letters X, P, I, which stand for CH, R, I (Christ), the first word of Saint Matthew's Gospel. These letters appear among networks of endless curves, spirals, plants, and animal forms—barbarian decorative devices adapted for the service of Christ.

This bronze **equestrian statuette** probably represents Charlemagne, the great German emperor who once ruled over most of Europe. Although the rider is shown in 9th-century costume, the sculptor was clearly inspired by ancient Roman art. Charlemagne did what he could to retrieve classical art from the obscurity it suffered during the barbarian invasions. It is said that the aging emperor wept at the thought of the menacing advances of Vikings along the borders of the empire.

A typical medieval monastery building is shown in a page from a 13th-century **manuscript**. In the doorway one monk signals the hour of prayer, sounding the bells in the tower to call others from their work of transcribing important documents. By such inspired work the monks helped preserve knowledge that was in danger of disappearing altogether during the barbaric invasions of Europe.

A carved wooden **animal head** from Norway, probably used in a pagan religious ceremony and found among the remains of a Viking ship, suggests the wild and ferocious spirit that the Church had to subdue to establish an orderly civilization.

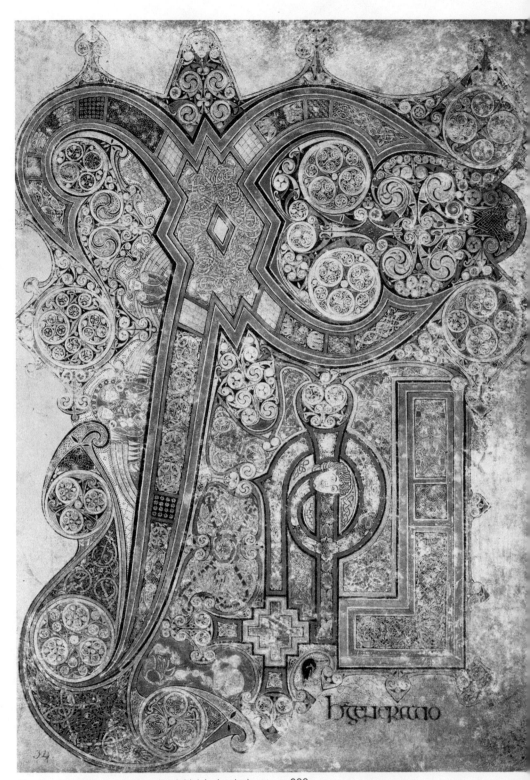

The Book of Kells, the Incarnation Initial, Ireland, about A.D. 800

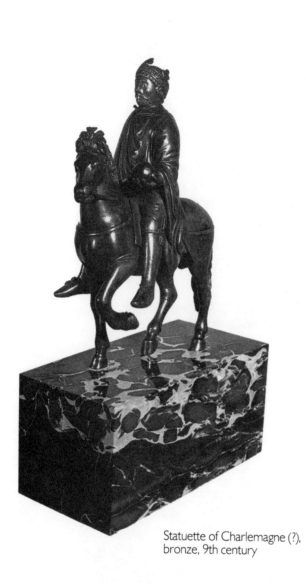

Statuette of Charlemagne (?),
bronze, 9th century

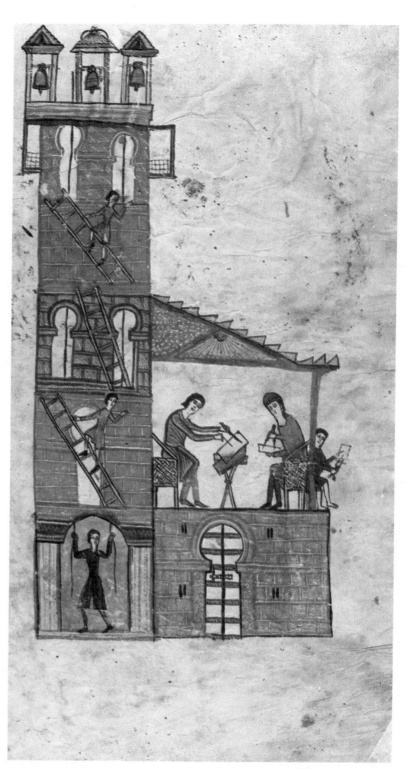

Medieval scriptorium in a manuscript from Spain, about A.D. 1220

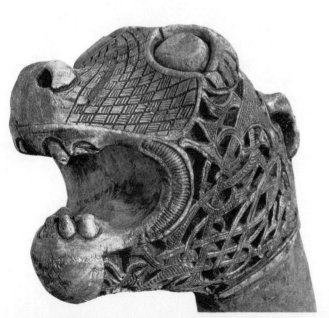

Viking carved animal head, wood, Norway, about A.D. 825

31

A **stained glass panel** from Canterbury cathedral in England pictures the three Magi (wise men) from the East, guided by a star, finding their way to Bethlehem to pay tribute to the newborn Christ child. The cathedral was started in the late 11th century following the Norman Conquest of England. It became the most famous destination for religious pilgrimages in that land, as told in Chaucer's *Canterbury Tales*.

The so-called **Bayeux Tapestry** is actually an embroidery. It is a pictorial account of the Norman Conquest of England in A.D. 1066. The entire epic story is told episode by episode in vivid detail. The warriors, helmeted and clad in chain mail, are vividly shown slaughtering one another. The figures were stitched on a linen background 230 feet long by a number of women working together not long after the conquest. It is one of the most unusual works of art from the Middle Ages.

Sculpture had a remarkable revival in the 11th and 12th centuries. Most of it consisted of Bible stories that decorated churches. The **capitals of columns** were favorite places for images that helped spread the gospel to congregations unable to read the Bible. The one reproduced here shows Daniel in the lions' den.

In some 11th- and 12th-century churches the stonecutters took advantage of every opportunity to chisel sermons in stone. With vivid imagination they illustrated religious subjects, as in **The Last Judgment** from a French church. In the very center, Christ sits in judgment. A group of pilgrims led by the Virgin approaches from his right. Below the pilgrims, the redeemed are pictured enjoying heavenly bliss. At the left of Christ, the damned are shown being shoved down the jaws of hell to be received by the devil and to suffer the unspeakable horrors that would be theirs everlastingly.

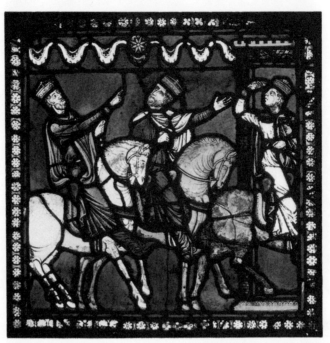

Stained glass window from Canterbury Cathedral, England, about 1200

The Last Judgment, Abbey, Church of Conques, France, 11th century

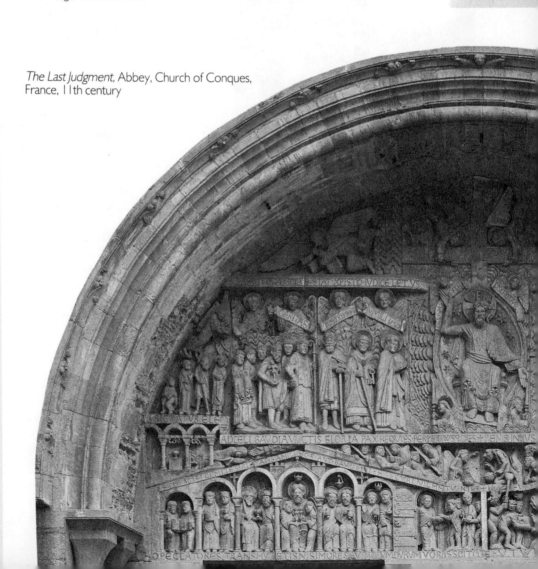

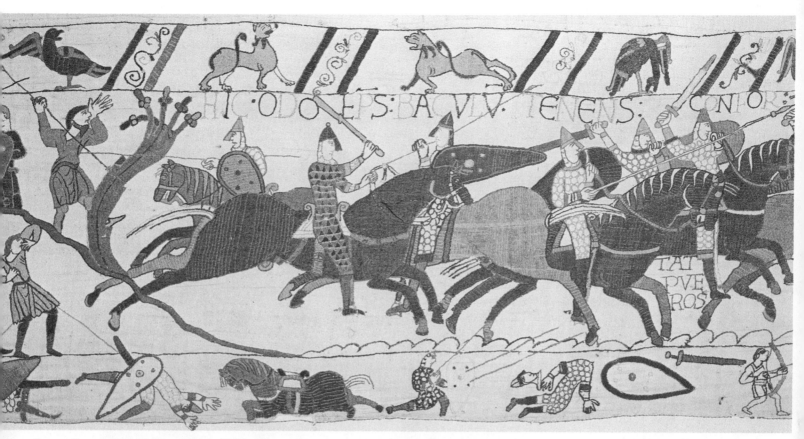

Bayeux Tapestry (detail), France, about 1073–83

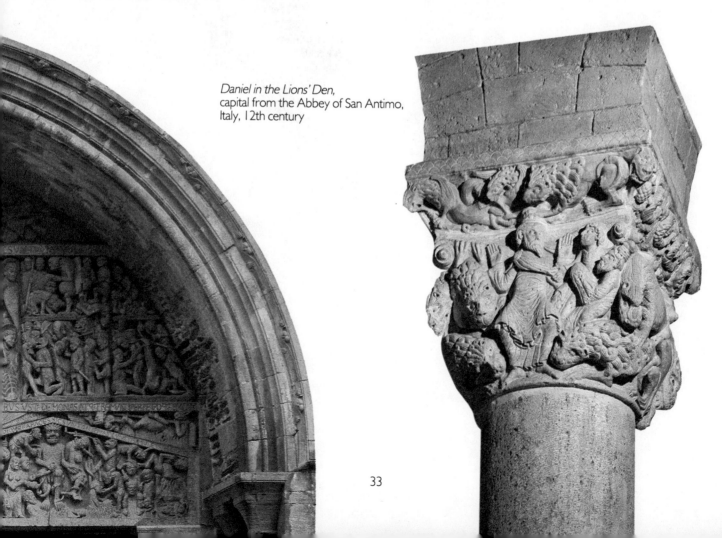

Daniel in the Lions' Den,
capital from the Abbey of San Antimo,
Italy, 12th century

33

By the end of the 13th century, **illuminated manuscripts** were less often produced in monasteries than in professional workshops. There, in the days before the invention of printing, scribes and illuminators put together elaborate volumes for the libraries of kings, princes, and nobles. One way or another, such books were accounts of Christian experience through the centuries as it was recorded or imagined. The picture reproduced on these pages is from a two-volume work produced in Brussels for Philippe the Good, the wealthy and powerful Duke of Burgundy, about 1459–62. It tells the story of the persecutions suffered by Christians from the time of Herod until 1276 and was illustrated by Loyset Liédet.

Before the 11th century, Muslims had overrun much of the Holy Land and controlled most of the shrines in the Near East that were sacred to Christians. In 1095 the French-born Pope Urban II delivered one of the most moving orations in history. He urged his countrymen to take up arms against the infidels who were desecrating these holy places. No available building was large enough to contain the audience that came to hear him preach, so he addressed the gathering in an open field. He assured his listeners that the undertaking he proposed would win them rewards on earth and in heaven. Thus was launched the first in a series of crusades that continued for several centuries.

Among the adversaries confronting the European knights were the Ottoman Turks, fierce warriors from farther east. One of their leaders, Suleiman, is here shown in battle with the Christians.

The two books in which this illustration appeared were finished just a few years after Constantinople fell to the Turks. This Christian city had defied the assaults by barbarians (and others) for more than a thousand years, and its downfall was a momentous event in the history of western civilization. The makers of these books probably had this event in mind when they pictured this earlier onslaught by Turkish warriors.

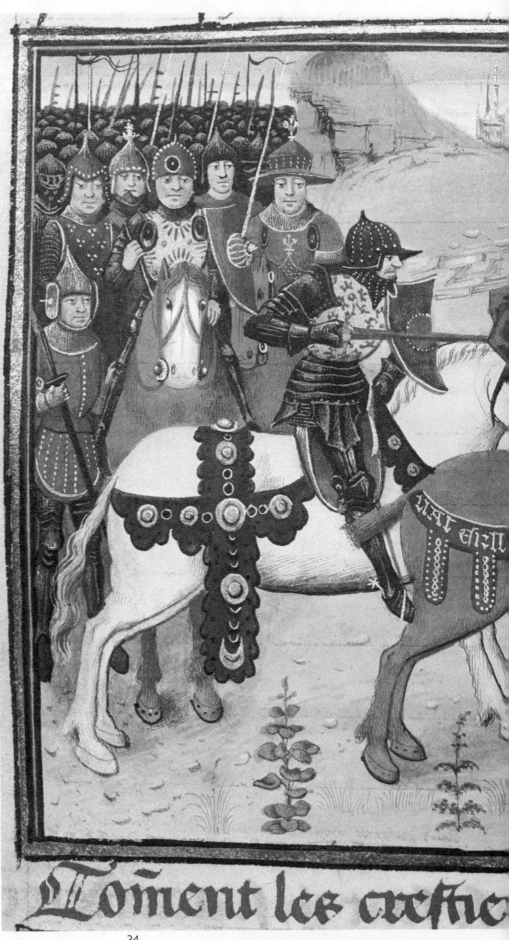

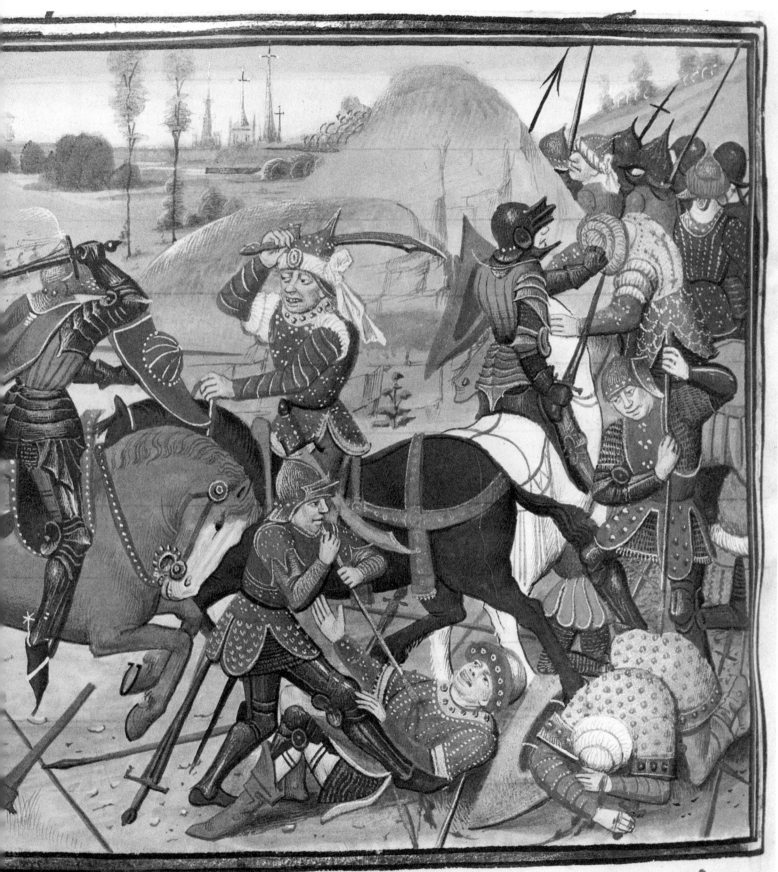

astrent la cite de magne · Et coment

35 David Aubert, *Chronicle of the Emperors*, about 1459–62

Early in the 15th century, three miniaturists called the Limbourg brothers created what is probably the most precious **illuminated manuscript** in the western world. It was commissioned by the enormously wealthy Duke of Berry, of the French province of Burgundy, brother of the king. Each of the manuscript's twelve main illustrations depicts one month of the year and shows typical occupations outdoors and in. These illustrations have been termed "the fountainhead of western landscape painting."

Such books of hours, as they are called, were abbreviated versions of the prayer books used by the clergy. The prayer books provided different prayers for each of the seven canonical hours of the day.

Among the most typical of the medieval arts were the magnificent **tapestries** that were woven to cover the walls of castles and cathedrals. This art reached a climax late in the 15th century. A famous example, one of a series that may have been designed to celebrate a marriage, depicts a beautiful lady examining her jewels at the entrance of an elaborate tent in a flowered field. At the right is a milk-white unicorn, a beast with a single horn in the middle of its forehead. People of the time believed in this legendary creature and considered it a symbol of Christ or chastity.

A finely sculpted and painted stone statue of the **Virgin and Child,** also made in Burgundy in the 15th century, shows Mary in a maternal role. Holding her young son in her lap, she quietly and attentively listens to his observations as he points to the open book before them. The artist has clearly suggested an intimate, deeply sympathetic relationship between the two.

In the last phase of medieval art, the subjects in sculpture and painting began to have individual characters that could have been based on the observation of human models. As we will see in the next chapter, this sort of realistic portrayal was an important characteristic of Renaissance art.

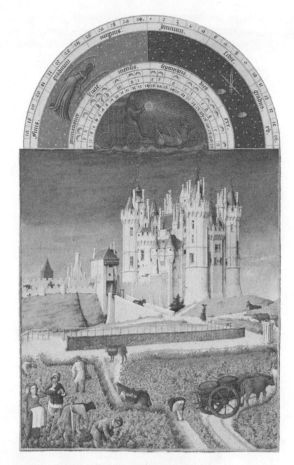

The Limbourg Brothers, "September" from *The Very Rich Hours of the Duke of Berry,* France, 1413–16

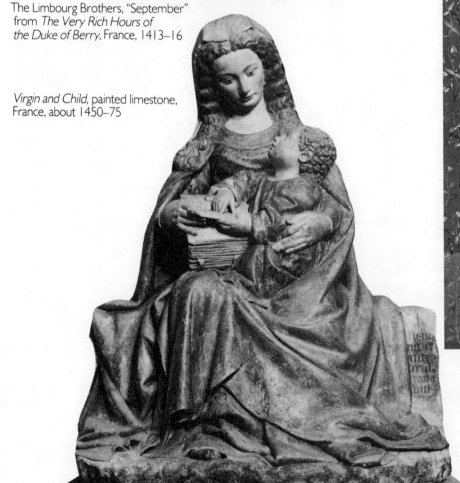

Virgin and Child, painted limestone, France, about 1450–75

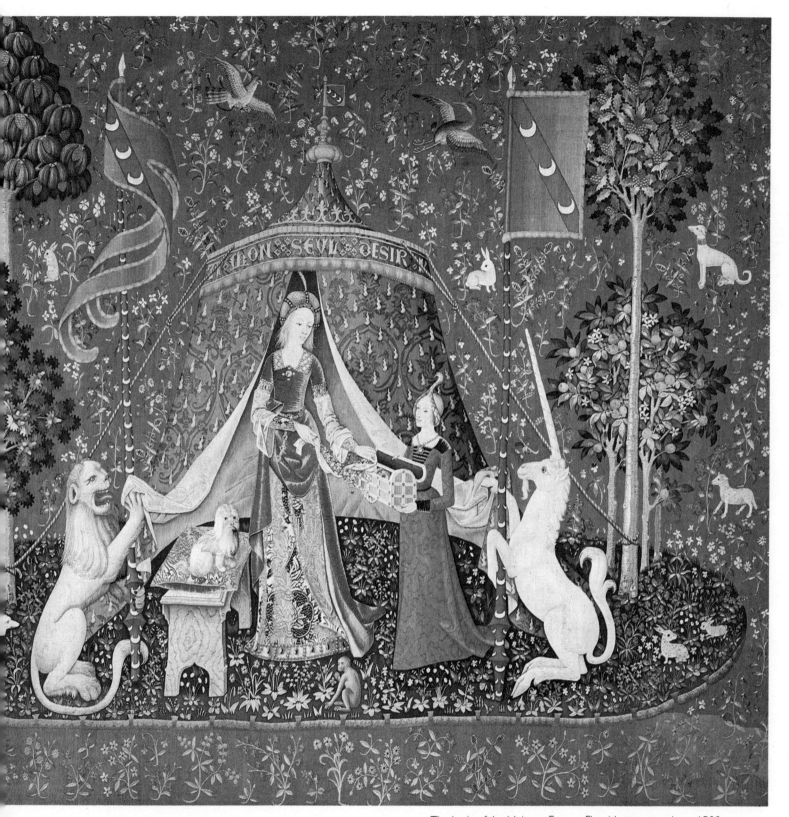

The Lady of the Unicorn, Franco-Flemish tapestry, about 1500

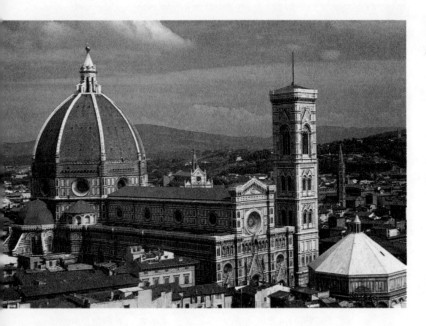

THE RENAISSANCE AND BAROQUE PERIOD

From about 1300 to 1600 great changes took place in European civilization. These first appeared in Italy while the Middle Ages was still running its course in northern Europe, then gradually spread over the entire continent and the British Isles. This period of three hundred years or so is called the Renaissance, a French word that means "rebirth." As we look back at that time, it appears that the minds and spirits of men were then truly reborn.

These were the years when navigators first found their way around the globe and when the printing press was developed—two giant steps forward for humankind. They were years when man saw himself as well as the world about him in a new and searching light. He sought ways of understanding the visible world as clearly as possible, and as had never before been done. In this search the arts played an important part.

Renaissance artists studied and practiced ways of making the flat surfaces they painted seem like windows looking out onto or into a real world of persons, places, and things. The artists attempted to show their subjects as they exist in space and actually appear to our eyes as we look here and there. They learned to do this through mathematical studies of perspective, discoveries that have had a great influence on the arts ever since. They investigated the nature of light and color to help shape the forms of their subjects as realistically as possible. They studied anatomy to learn how the play of underlying bones, muscles, and sinews accounts for the attitudes of a human body at rest or in action. (Leonardo da Vinci, among other artists, dissected corpses to learn how the body is constructed.)

Few true portraits were painted in the Middle Ages. But as the Renaissance advanced it produced many likenesses of clearly recognizable individuals, setting standards for the ages to come. Sculptors created figures in the round that looked all but alive. They found models in sculptures surviving from ancient Greece and Rome, which they admired and studied.

Renaissance culture was, in fact, deeply rooted in the classical past. Princes and popes surrounded themselves with scholars who became familiar with long-neglected writings of the early Greeks and Romans. This revival of classical learning was a dominating force in the development of Renaissance culture. With newly invented scientific instruments, Renaissance men explored the heavens to determine the true place of humankind under the sun amid the countless galaxies. This they did. Wise men of the time concluded that man was the measure of all things—as the Greeks had done almost 2,000 years before. The individual person was all important.

Italy led in shaping Renaissance art partly because more

examples of classical art and architecture had survived there than in any other land. But there was more to it than that. The wealth accumulated from its active commerce gave Italy the funds to sponsor the arts on a large scale.

Italy was not then a nation. It was a land of independent city-states, ruled by powerful merchant princes who often warred with one another. To fight their battles these rulers hired troops assembled and led by condottieri, or paid officers, who sold their services to the highest bidders. The ruling families also competed for the services of the finest artists of the day and became their patrons.

During the Middle Ages the artist was thought of as little more than a capable workman, not a person whose name was worth remembering. Now such great masters as Leonardo da Vinci, Michelangelo, Raphael, and Titian were considered to be individuals of genius, worthy companions of the rich and powerful patrons for whom they created masterpieces. Their names will never be forgotten. For the first time the history of art was, indeed, becoming a history of great artists. Some of the best of these are recorded in this book.

Country by country, the influence of the Italian Renaissance spread over Europe. In each country or region, that influence was expressed according to the different traditions and circumstances of the area. Artists from northern Europe came to Italy to learn what they could in that land and to carry the borrowed ideas back home. The German artist Albrecht Dürer crossed and recrossed the Alps and introduced Renaissance art to his country. Italian artists also visited the north to exercise their special talents there. So, at a summons from the Emperor Francis I, da Vinci went to France, where he died in a château on the banks of the Loire River.

This give and take of talents and ideas broadened the whole range of art. A better understanding of what had been and what could be done freed the artist to explore new paths that led in many directions. In the 16th century the Reformation, a religious revolution that began in Germany, split Europe into Protestant and Catholic countries. Many Protestants felt that religious art was a form of idol worship and would have none of it in their churches or their homes. Cut off from the patronage of the Church, artists in Protestant Europe turned to nonreligious subjects—landscapes, still lifes, scenes of daily life, and portraits, of course. Some artists, when they had no commissions for a specific work of art, painted subjects of their own choice, which they put up for sale. From then on this sort of speculation became more the rule than the exception.

All the greatest masters of the Renaissance had died before the year 1600. In their work they had brought the ideals of Renaissance art to a point of unsurpassable perfection. A new generation of artists would have to discover other standards of excellence if the arts were to move forward. This they did in different ways. Some attracted attention by exaggerating the proportions of the human body in a strange manner and arranging their subjects in unusual postures. (They have become known as Mannerists.) Other artists used color and light in new ways to create special effects.

In the 17th century, as the Reformation continued to find more converts in northern Europe, a rebellious young Italian artist named Caravaggio began to paint in a fresh way. In his canvases he used light in a way that made them resemble dramatic stage sets. The actors in his scenes were painted from life, intensely real and active under the spotlight. His sort of theatrical presentation made a deep impression on the artists of France, Spain, and the Netherlands.

Holland at this time was swarming with good artists and with well-to-do citizens who bought their work. Although his career had its ups and downs, Rembrandt was the greatest of these painters. The dramatic play of light and shade in his works is a remote development of Caravaggio's earlier inventions.

In branching out from the Renaissance style, artists of the 1600s took such a variety of paths that it is hard to find a single term to classify the work of the century. Some use the term "baroque style" to describe the major output of those years.

About 1340 **Ambrogio Lorenzetti** painted a scene that he called *Good Government in the City and the Country* (a detail is shown here). It represents Siena, then a powerful and prosperous city-state, and the rolling hills and cultivated fields of the surrounding countryside. The scene hums with activities of all kinds. Men work on the roof of one of the buildings; merchants set out their wares for sale; women dance in the streets. A hunting party sets out toward fields where peasants till the earth. Everything is directly observed from life as the artist knew it. It was the first landscape of its kind since Roman times.

Simone Martini, an important artist of the early 1300s, was less interested in realism than in the colorful designs he could invent from what he knew of the world around him. One of his well-known paintings shows the powerful condottiero (hired warrior) Guidoricci da Fogliano after a great victory over rebellious nobles. He and his horse are outfitted in colorful embroidered robes as they advance through a fanciful landscape of fortified castles. (The castle at the right is equipped with a newly developed mechanism for hurling rocks at an enemy.) A military camp is shown at the far right.

Giotto was one of the most important painters in the history of art. At the beginning of the Italian Renaissance, around 1300, he led the way toward a new manner of painting that transformed the flat surface he worked on into what seemed like an open space filled with people. In his painting of Judas about to betray Jesus by kissing him, the figures appear like actual human bodies that one might reach out and touch and walk around. Their faces clearly show their feelings as they stare intently at each other. This kind of realism in art had not been known since the days of ancient Rome. After the flat, patterned images of medieval painting, this was a revolutionary rediscovery.

Giotto's fame quickly spread throughout Italy. Great men of his time hailed his genius. And artists who followed him, proudly signed themselves "disciple of Giotto, the good master."

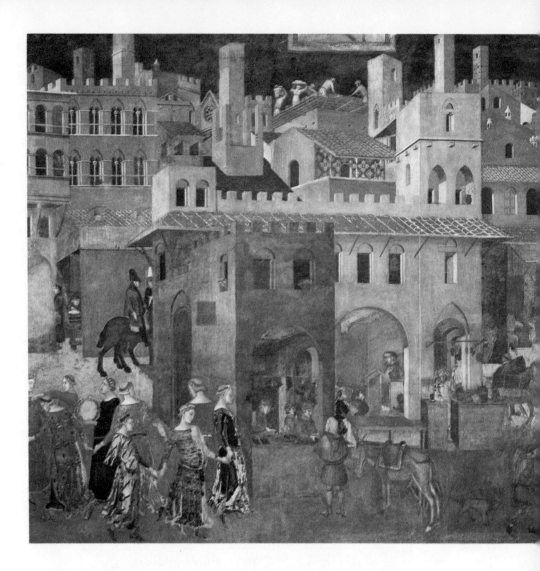

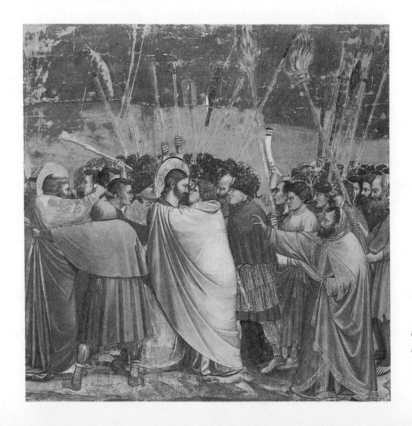

Giotto, *The Kiss of Judas,* about 1310

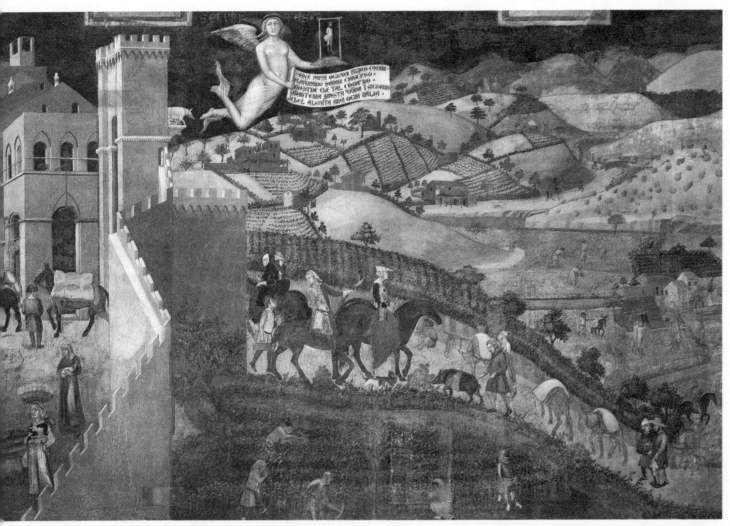

Ambrogio Lorenzetti, *Good Government in the City and the Country* (detail), 1338-40

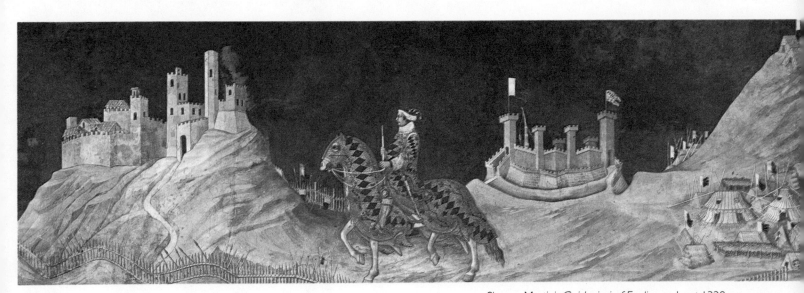

Simone Martini, *Guidoricci of Fogliano,* about 1328

In 1459 **Benozzo Gozzoli** was hired to decorate the walls of the chapel in the great Medici palace in Florence. At the time this artist's works were in great demand. On one of the walls he painted the story of the Magi, the three wise men who came from the East, guided by the star of Bethlehem, to bring tribute to the newborn Christ child. In his painting Gozzoli chose to represent this biblical story as a contemporary event. He showed it as a splendid procession led by members of the Medici family and other important, well-dressed people of the time, winding its way through an invented landscape down from a distant hilltop.

At the head of the procession, riding a white horse, is a handsome youth, possibly the young Lorenzo de Medici. He wears the golden robes and red hose he wore at an oriental festival given in Florence. Cosimo de Medici, father of Lorenzo, follows on the back of a plodding mule and is attended by a black page. The Magi themselves, almost lost in the crowd, are portraits of princes alive at the time, including the emperor of Byzantium and the patriarch of Constantinople, both of whom had recently paid a state visit to Italy. Gozzoli also included his own portrait in the crowd of followers.

The background is enlivened by huntsmen, animals, and birds amid exotic flowering plants. Gozzoli turned the wall into a theatrical pageant, which was his intention. It is altogether a gay and glittering spectacle.

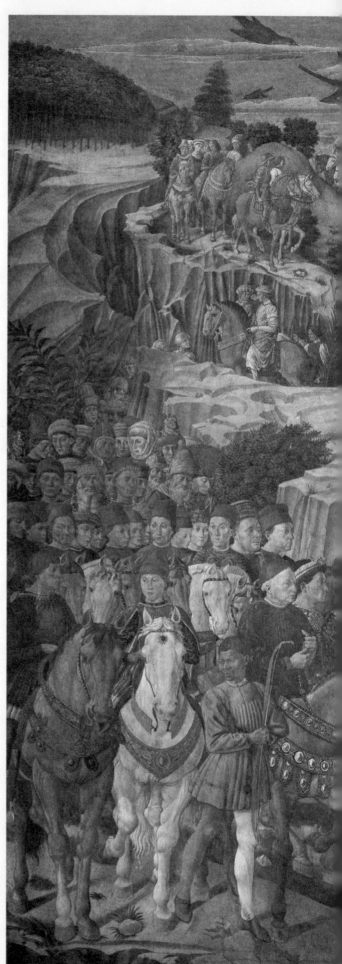

Benozzo Gozzoli, *Procession of the Magi with Lorenzo the Magnificent and His Retinue*, 1450

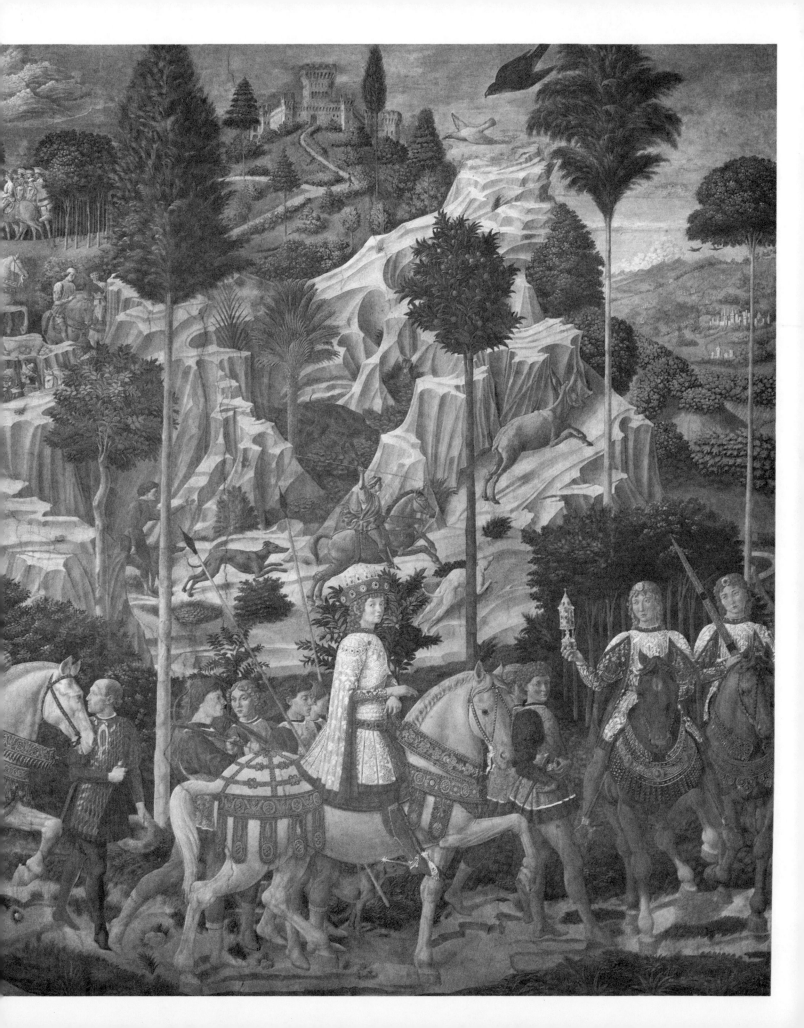

One of the greatest of all Renaissance artists was the sculptor **Donatello.** His *David* was the first life-size, bronze, freestanding nude since antiquity. Donatello shows David not as a heavily muscled hero, but as a lithe and graceful adolescent. It was a completely original creation. Like Giotto a century earlier, Donatello won great fame in his lifetime. The outright, expertly modeled realism of his works had a profound influence on painters as well as sculptors.

Another artist who worked in Florence for the Medici was **Sandro Botticelli.** (Botticelli was a nickname that, literally translated, means "little barrel.") He was not a Realist like Donatello or Ghirlandaio. His paintings seem more like poetic dreams than anything true to life. One of his masterpieces, the famous *Birth of Venus,* shows the pagan goddess Venus being born from the sea, true to ancient Greek myth. Botticelli shows her riding the waves on a gleaming shell as she is blown ashore by gentle breezes. The painter created a type of grace and beauty that was entirely his own, as was the smooth, linear elegance with which he described his subject.

The painter **Domenico Ghirlandaio** was a somewhat younger contemporary of Donatello's. He also was a Realist. His double portrait of an ugly old man with a deformed nose and his handsome, curly haired little grandson is one of his best-remembered paintings. The faces of the two seem so real and the affection they share is so tenderly expressed that the picture leaves an unforgettable image in one's mind.

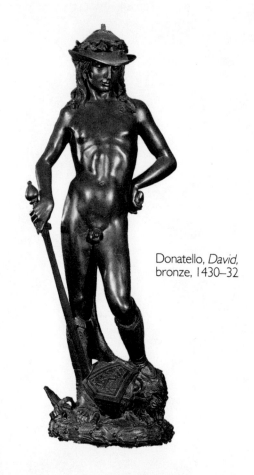

Donatello, *David,* bronze, 1430–32

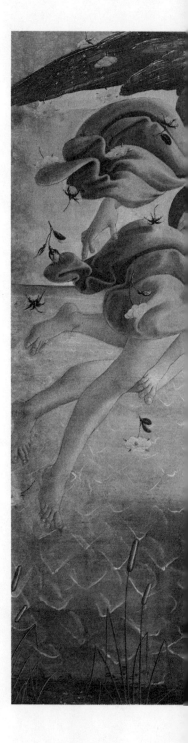

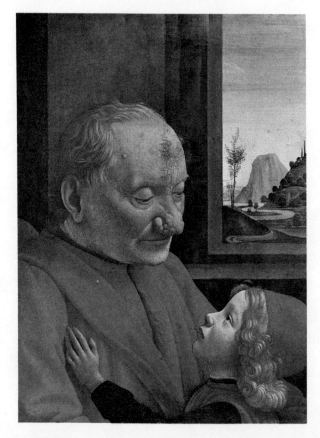

Domenico Ghirlandaio, *An Old Man and His Grandson,* about 1480

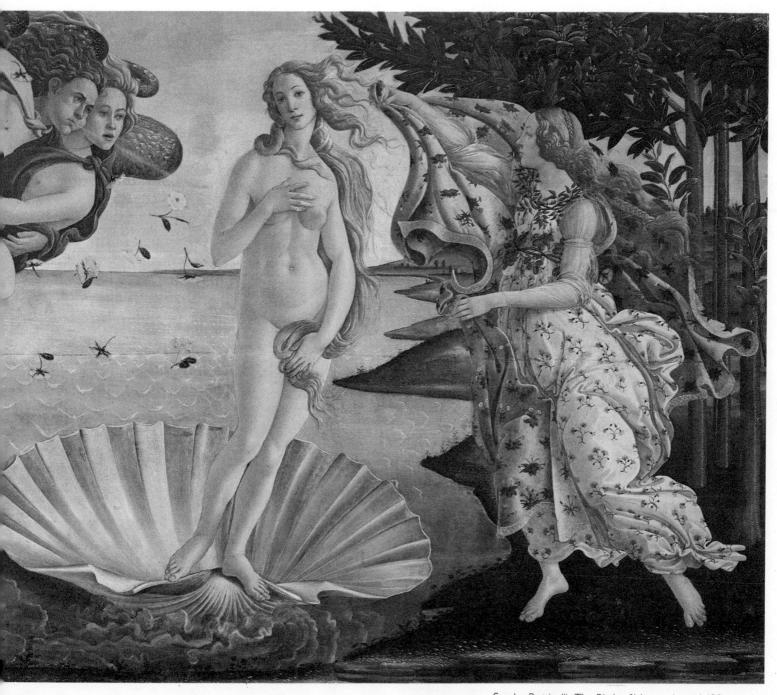

Sandro Botticelli, *The Birth of Venus*, about 1480

Michelangelo Buonarroti, painter, sculptor, poet, and architect, was one of the greatest artists of all time. The first work in which he showed his remarkable skill as a sculptor was this *Pietà,* which he cut in marble in about 1498 when he was still in his twenties. This was going to be, claimed the Roman banker who commissioned the work, "more beautiful than any work in marble to be seen in Rome." And so it is. Some critics complained that the Virgin seemed too young to be the mother of the grown man she held in her lap. Michelangelo retorted that "chastity enjoys eternal youth." Ten years later he undertook to paint, single-handed, the story of Creation on the ceiling of the Sistine Chapel in the Vatican. This was a gigantic accomplishment that took him six years, and during which he had to paint lying on his back on a scaffold, looking upward.

One of the most striking details in this vast fresco is the moment when Adam, a vigorous and muscular figure, is called to life by the mere touch of God's finger. In his vision of this creation, Michelangelo performed a miracle of the painter's art.

Masaccio has been called "Giotto reborn." He was, in fact, the first painter to develop Giotto's early three-dimensional realism to a finished form. *The Tribute Money* (a detail is shown here) was his masterpiece. Here, in the presence of his disciples, Christ sends Saint Peter to fetch from the mouth of a fish the tribute money due the Roman tax collectors. All the figures in this composition appear to be active, live individual beings. We can imagine the firm structure of their bodies beneath their clothing and imagine from their facial expressions and their attitudes what sort of men they were. Masaccio painted this picture in 1427, when he was 26. He died the next year, ending a very short but brilliant career.

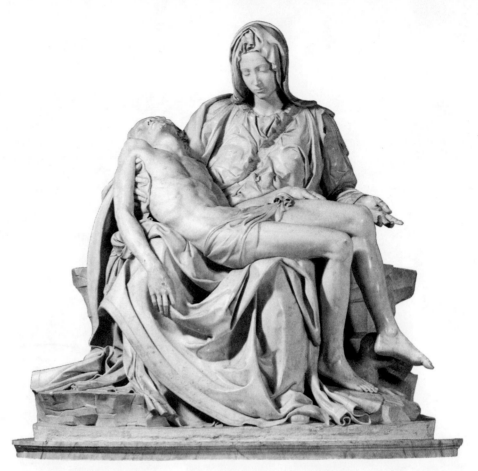

Michelangelo Buonarroti, *Pietà,* marble, 1498–1500

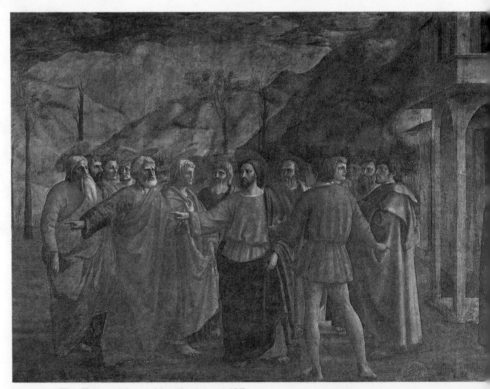

Masaccio, *The Tribute Money* (detail), about 1427

Michelangelo Buonarroti, fresco from the Sistine Chapel (detail), 1508–

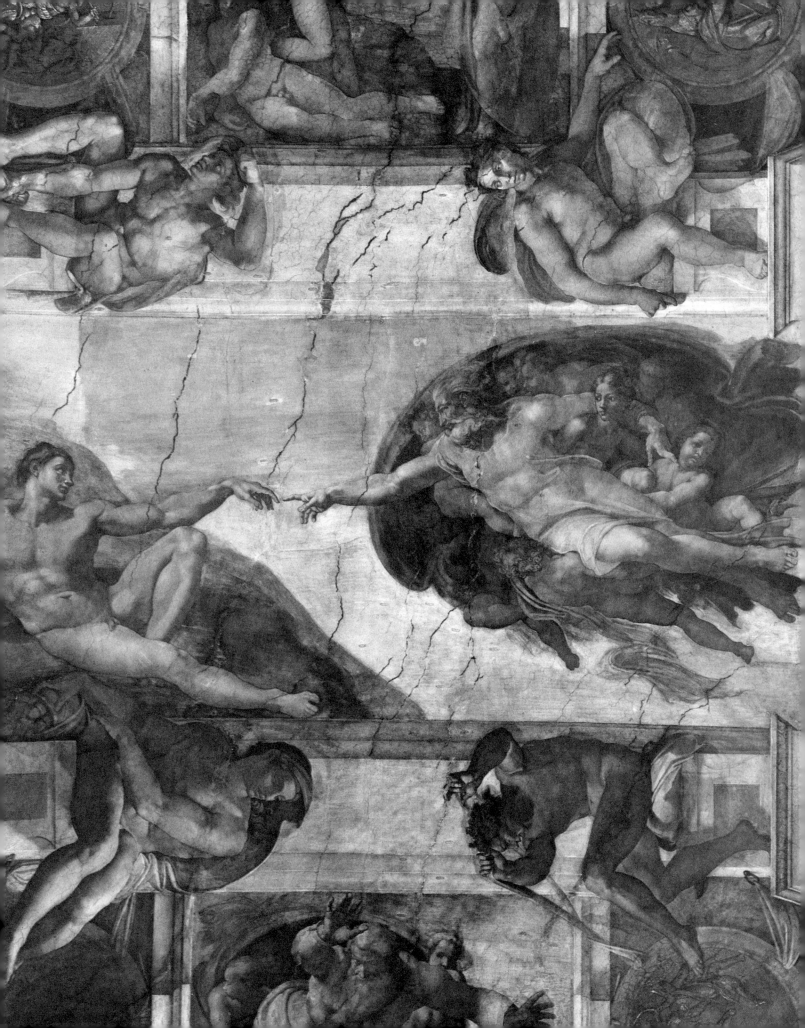

In painting the ceiling of the Sistine Chapel, **Michelangelo** worked from detailed drawings he made for each figure. One drawing, of a sibyl (a woman regarded as a prophetess by the ancient Greeks and Romans), shows how well the artist knew and could picture the interplay of muscles. No one before him since the ancient Greeks had so clearly observed and demonstrated the workings of the human body.

Giovanni Paolo Negroli was one of the great Italian armorers of the 16th century, when such highly ornamented metalwork reached a height of perfection. This ceremonial helmet was hammered out of a single piece of steel; the decoration was chiseled in the cold metal and then partly gilded. At the back is a holder for a plume. It was made for one of the Medicis.

Michelangelo called **Benvenuto Cellini** the "greatest goldsmith of whom the world has ever heard." The only major work in precious metal by Cellini that has survived is this saltcellar he made for the King of France. Since salt comes from the sea, Cellini created the figure of Neptune (god of the sea) as guardian of the container. The elongated figures recall the Mannerist paintings of the time.

The last and greatest work by **Andrea del Verrocchio**, a goldsmith, sculptor, and painter, was the large equestrian statue of Bartolommeo Colleoni, a soldier of fortune, or condottiere, who fought both for and against Venice. In his adventures he made a fortune, which he left to Venice with the condition that a statue in his honor be placed in the main square. There it still stands—the horse almost quivering with energy; the rider in armor, fierce with warlike determination.

In his great work on architecture, the ancient Roman Vitruvius stated that "the measurements of a man are arranged by Nature thus. . . . The span of a man's outstretched arms is equal to his height." In one of his innumerable drawings Michelangelo's older contemporary **Leonardo da Vinci** graphically demonstrated that definition of the proportions of an ideal body.

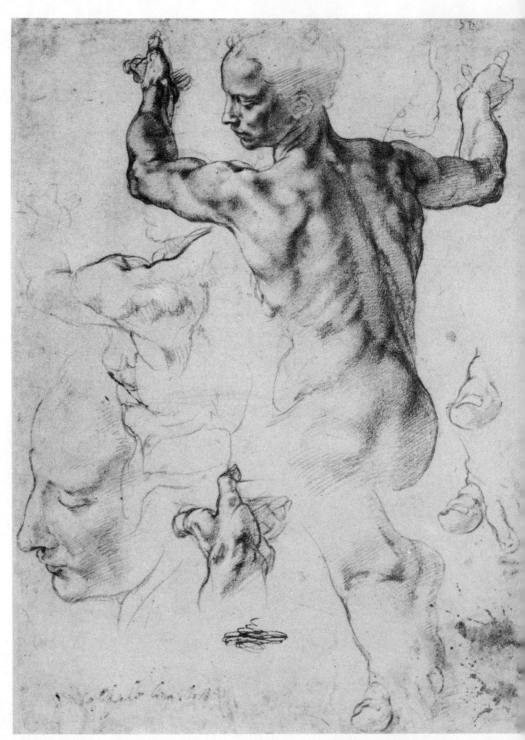

Michelangelo Buonarroti, *Studies for the Libyan Sibyl*, 1511–12

48

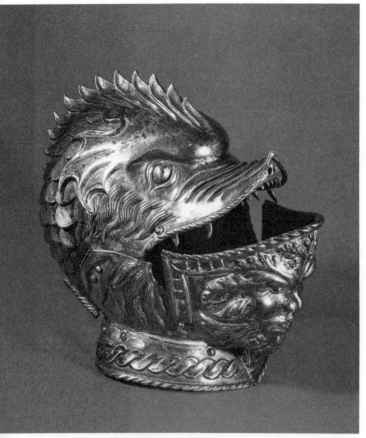

Giovanni Paolo Negroli, ornamental helmet, steel, 1545–50

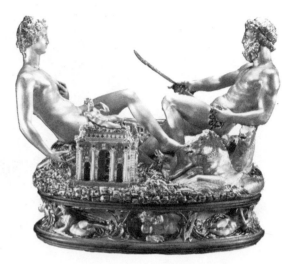

Benvenuto Cellini, saltcellar of Francis I,
gold with enamel, 1539–43

Andrea del Verrocchio,
*Equestrian Monument of
Bartolommeo Colleoni* (detail),
bronze, about 1483–88

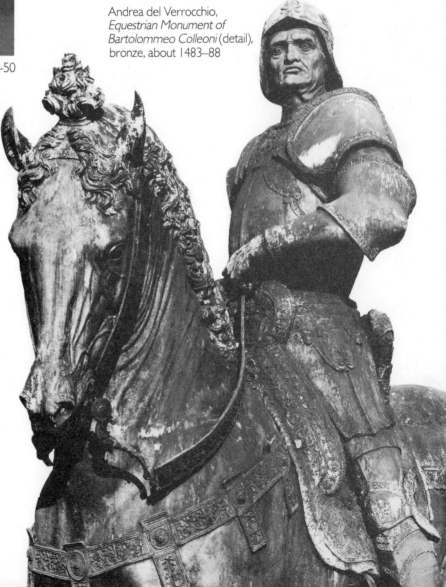

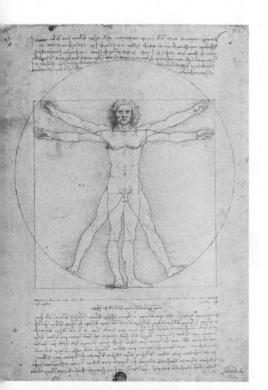

Leonardo da Vinci, *Vitruvian Man*, about 1490

Leonardo da Vinci is often referred to as the greatest genius who ever lived and the first modern man. In his sketchbooks he drew designs for an incredible number of things that foretold inventions that became widely accepted only in modern times, from airplanes to pile drivers, from three-speed transmission gears to armored tanks. The list is almost endless. He dissected bodies of people and animals and made the first true anatomical drawings.

He considered painting the greatest of the arts, and the few of his own works that have survived are among the most famous masterpieces of all time. His *Last Supper* and the *Mona Lisa* are familiar to almost everyone. Countless reproductions have been made of them for distribution around the world. Both paintings are celebrated for their realism and for the unique way that da Vinci blended the shapes and colors of the subjects and backgrounds in complete harmony. We wonder what the quietly smiling Mona Lisa is thinking of. For centuries this has remained a haunting mystery.

Along with da Vinci, Michelangelo, and Titian, **Raphael** was one of the foremost painters of the Italian High Renaissance. His religious pictures brought Renaissance art to a climax. His masterpiece was the *School of Athens*, a wall painting commissioned by the pope for the Vatican, which was finished about 1510. It is one of several in the same room, a series that represents an ideal combination of pagan and Christian themes in art.

In the center of Raphael's composition, Plato and Aristotle lead a discussion of ideas with a group of ancient pagan philosophers and scientists. Raphael has managed successfully to place some fifty figures (one is a self-portrait) on his painted stage. In niches on either side of the central figures, he painted gigantic statues of Apollo and Minerva.

Raphael's art commanded great admiration (and still does). One 16th-century witness reported that when Michelangelo was obliged to stop in the street to make room for Raphael's entourage, he remarked, "You travel accompanied by your court like a prince."

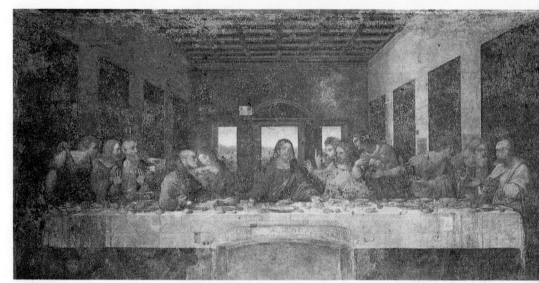

Leonardo da Vinci, *The Last Supper*, about 1495–98

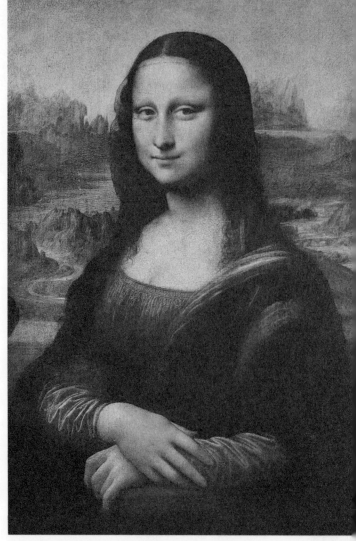

Leonardo da Vinci, *Mona Lisa*, about 1503–1505

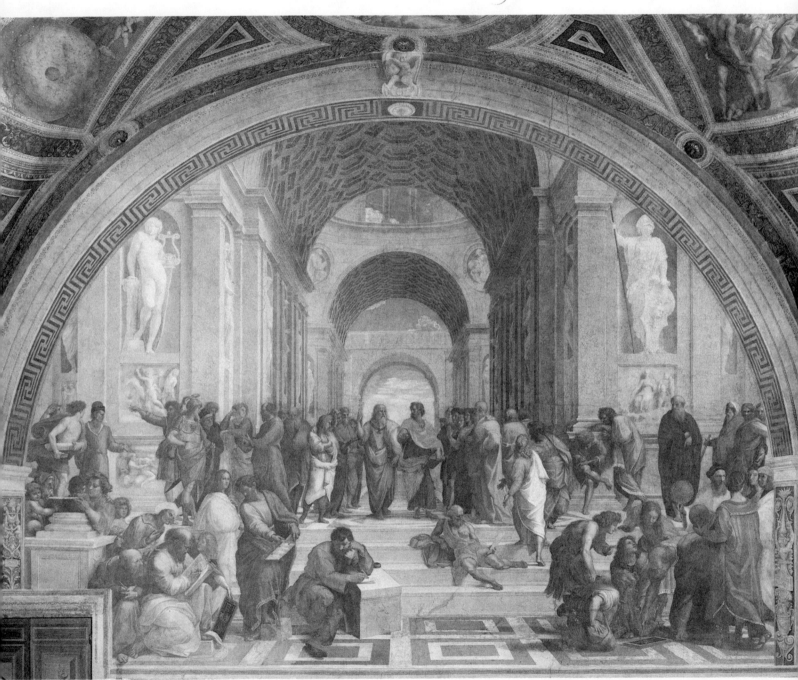

Raphael, *School of Athens*, 1510–11

Titian was one of the four greatest painters of the High Renaissance in Italy. He lived to be either 90 or 100 years old (it is not certain which) and was busy at his profession right up to his death in 1576. He was a Venetian and a supreme colorist. He enjoyed the esteem of popes and princes, who competed for his services and rewarded him well. At Pope Paul III's request he painted portraits of the pope more than once.

As explained in the introduction to this chapter, **Caravaggio**'s best paintings were intensely realistic and at the same time dramatic in a new way that deeply impressed artists who followed him. He led a very irregular, lawless life, killed at least one man, and was rarely out of trouble with the authorities for his brawling and his immoral conduct.

In *The Calling of St. Matthew*, he placed the crucial event in a common tavern. As Christ points to Matthew, the figures seated at the table emerge from the gloomy interior as though illuminated by a celestial spotlight.

Giorgione was a Venetian artist who died at the early age of 32. Only a few paintings are firmly identified as his. Among them is *The Tempest*—one of the most unusual works of the Renaissance. The title was made up long after his death and no one knows for sure what the painting means. A nude woman sits on the grass suckling a child while a clothed man stands at a slight distance watching her. In the background, storm clouds gather over a nearby city. No matter what it represents, it is a beautiful and haunting painting.

Agnolo Bronzino's *Portrait of a Young Man with Lute* is a typical example of this artist's work. He was at his best, as here, in painting likenesses of elegant men and women, reserved in manner, whose figures were elongated in the Mannerist tradition. He became court painter to the Medici.

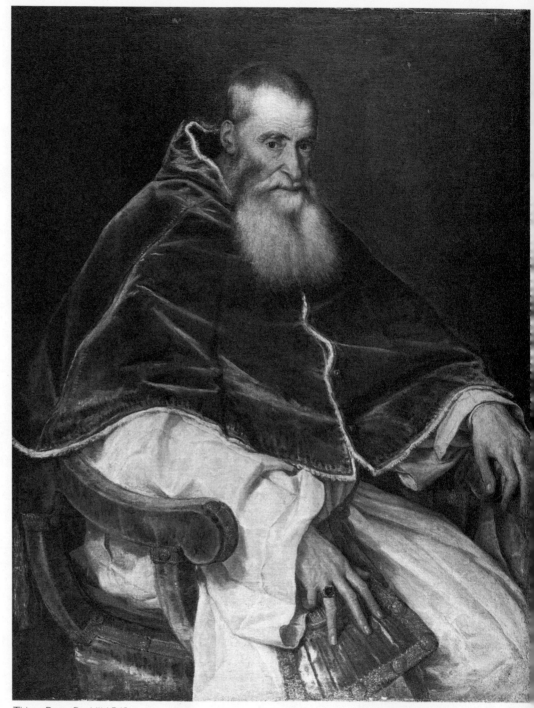

Titian, *Pope Paul III*, 1543

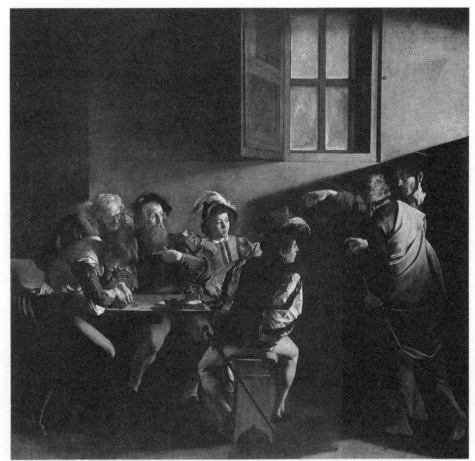

Caravaggio, *The Calling of St. Matthew,* about 1599

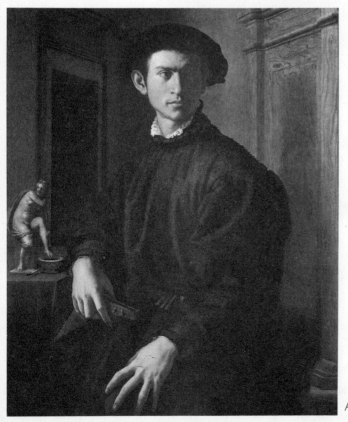

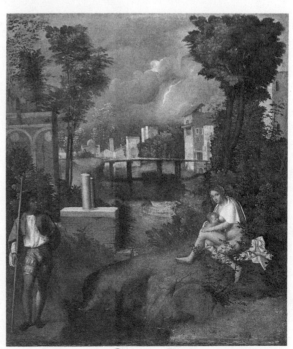

Giorgione, *The Tempest,* about 1505

Agnolo Bronzino, *Portrait of a Young Man with Lute,* 1532–40

In the 15th century a Flemish artist who painted in oils, **Jan van Eyck**, produced a gigantic altarpiece for the cathedral in Ghent, Belgium, perhaps helped by his older brother, Hubert. It is one of the masterpieces of the age. It is made up of many separate panels and only a small portion of it can be shown on these pages. In the center of one panel Christ is shown as a lamb surrounded by angels. Van Eyck and some of his contemporaries started a trend in realism that was typical of Flemish painting for scores of years thereafter. Everything is depicted with minute precision, although the giant size of the whole painting makes the details difficult to appreciate except at very close range.

Jan van Eyck had an international reputation. He served as a confidential ambassador for Philippe the Good, Duke of Burgundy, who wrote that he "would never find a man equally to his liking nor so outstanding in his art and science."

About the same time, while Donatello, Masaccio, and other great artists were mastering the Renaissance style in Italy, very gifted artists were perfecting quite different styles in the Low Countries to the north. No one can say for sure who painted the **Campin Altarpiece** in about 1425. It may have been the Flemish painter Robert Campin, about whom very little is known. Whoever he was, he was among the earliest artists to use oil-based paints. This helped him develop new ways of blending colors. It has been the painter's principal medium ever since.

In the Campin Altarpiece every element of the picture, small or large, clearly defines the everyday appearance of things—the gleam of copper and brass, the surface of the figured pottery pitcher with its spray of lilies, the solid carved stone and wood. But it is above all a religious painting, the first to show the angel Gabriel announcing the birth of Christ in a fully furnished domestic interior.

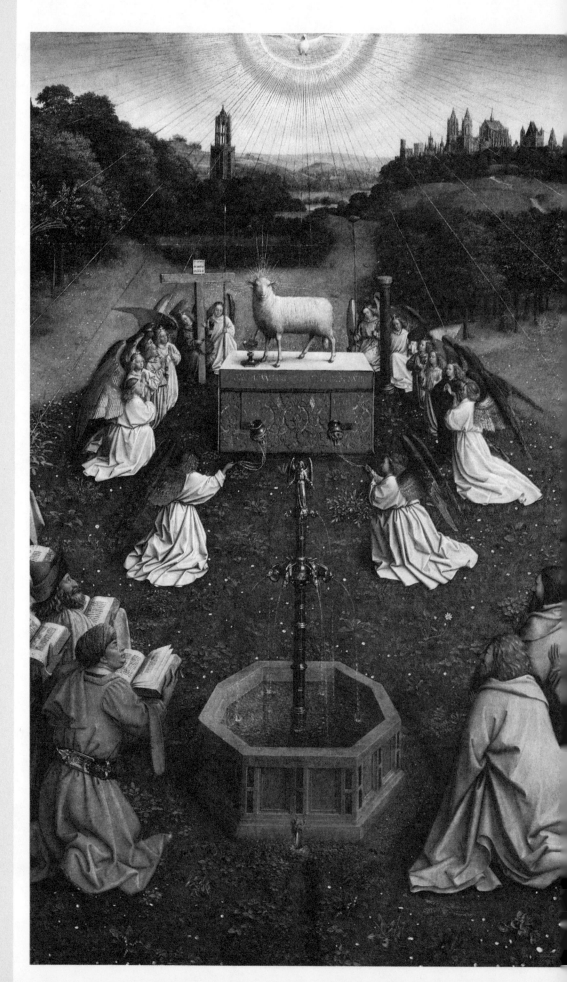

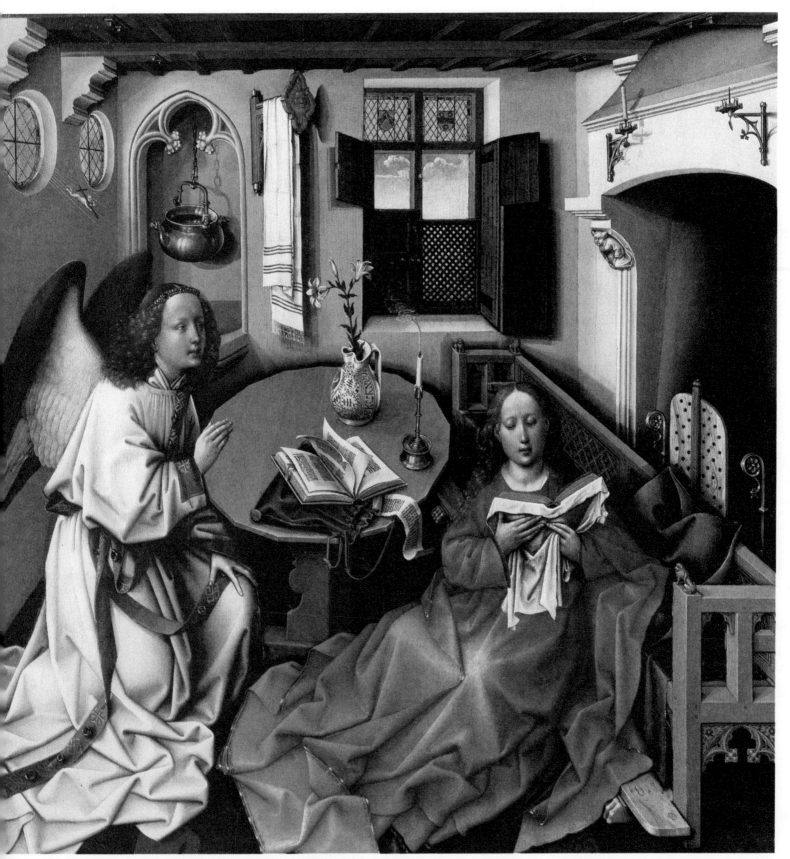

Robert Campin, *The Annunciation,* central panel of the Campin Altarpiece, about 1425–28

and Hubert van Eyck, Ghent Altarpiece, detail of central panel, 1432

Albrecht Dürer was the greatest early German artist. He was also one of the major artists of the Renaissance and the Reformation. He has been called the northern Leonardo, for he was a learned man in many fields in addition to being an outstanding painter.

A very vain and handsome man, he painted many self-portraits. The example reproduced here shows him elegantly garbed in the highest fashion with his carefully curled long hair falling to his shoulders. On a very productive visit to Italy he had seen how highly artists were esteemed in that country. Thereafter he thought of himself as a true aristocrat simply because of his inborn and well-developed talents rather than because of his pedigree.

The Garden of Delights by the Dutch artist **Hieronymus Bosch,** painted about 1500, may never be explained satisfactorily—at least it has not yet been, although many wise scholars have guessed at its meaning. The painting has also been titled *The Garden of Lust*. It is a painting in three parts, of which the central and largest section is shown here. It is filled with, among other things, naked young men and women engaged in very strange antics. For the other figures, the artist seems to have mixed up the genes of humans, other mammals, birds, and serpents and in his imagination has bred weird hybrids never seen on earth or anyplace else except in the wildest of dreams. The gloomy king of Spain, Philip II, found the painting intriguing enough to buy it for his royal collection.

The painting of a *Moneylender and His Wife* is the finest work of **Quentin Metsys,** a Flemish artist. Metsys had a strong interest in portraying the common man and his surroundings in minute detail. In this painting the convex mirror in the foreground reflects what is probably the artist's self-portrait. Every small object in the scene can be clearly identified, as though we were actually in the room with the busy couple.

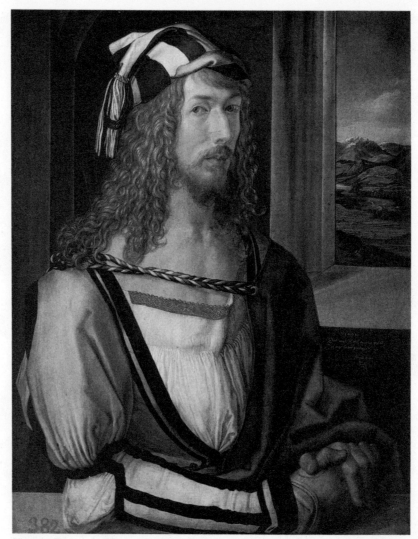

Albrecht Dürer, *Self-Portrait,* 1498

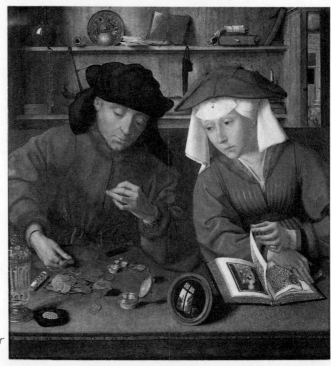

Quentin Metsys, *The Moneylender and His Wife,* 1514

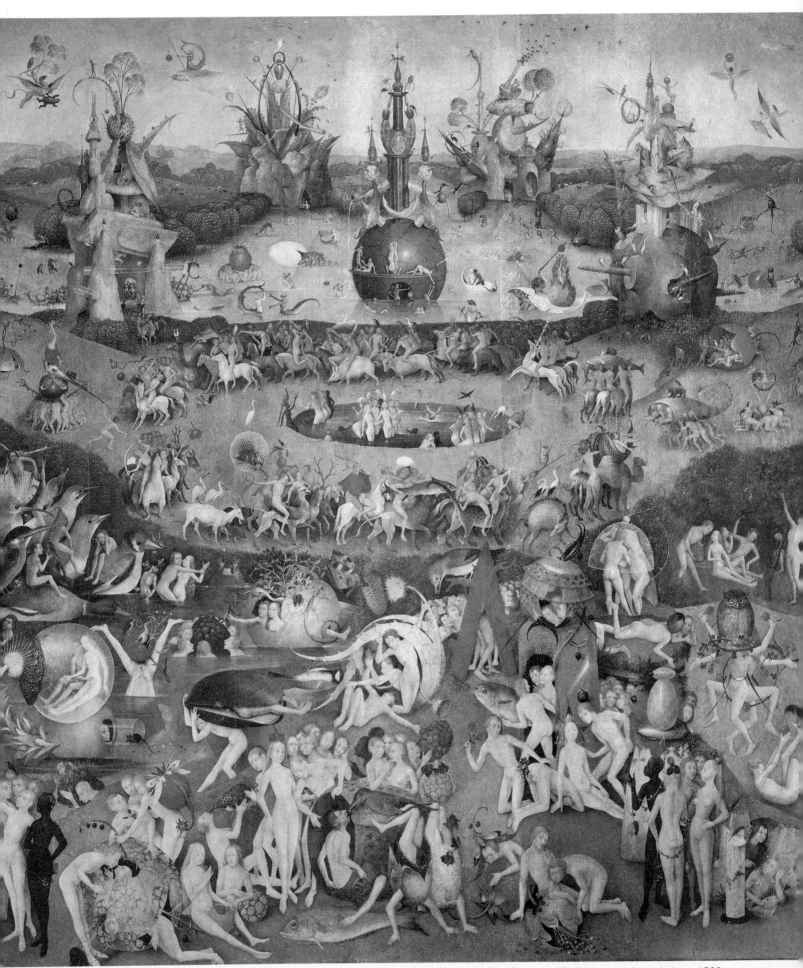

Hieronymus Bosch, *The Garden of Delights*, central panel, about 1500

In *Peasant Wedding*, painted about 1565, **Pieter Bruegel the Elder** provides an intimate look at life in the Low Countries. Here stout-bodied, coarsely clothed Flemish peasants, entertained by musicians, show a healthy delight in a wedding feast being held in a barn. In the center of the picture, the bride sits quietly, grinning contentedly, with a sort of crown hanging above her head. Bruegel neither prettified nor ridiculed his rustic characters. He painted the scene "as it was."

Jan Vermeer was one of the "Little Dutchmen," so called because of their attention to the small details of their subjects. His work reflects, almost as in a mirror, quiet moments in the domestic life of the prosperous, respectable middle class of Holland in the 17th century. Like his other paintings, *The Artist in His Studio* takes us into a well-furnished interior bathed in light coming from a window at the left. This painting was made almost a century after *Peasant Wedding*. Also, as in Vermeer's other work, he shows us an instant in time when all action is suspended so that we can closely examine everything in the room as the "actors" pause as though under a magic spell.

Jan Steen was a cheerful reporter of 17th-century Dutch life. In his painting *Merry Company* he and his own family portray a group of tipsy revelers enjoying themselves without restraint. One feels that the artist took as much joy in painting the scene as the merrymakers did in their antics. The fact that Steen ran an inn gave him ample opportunity to study the appearance and behavior of the types he pictured here. We often associate Dutch 17th-century art with this mood of gaiety and good living.

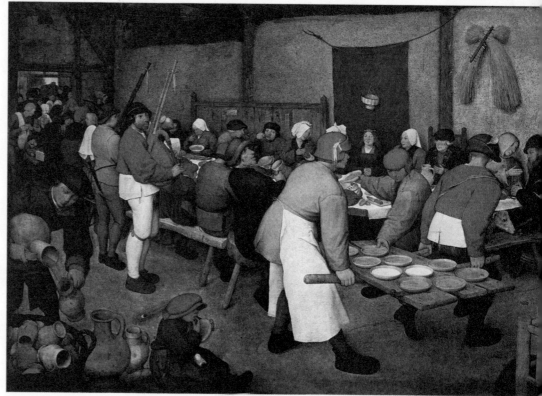

Pieter Bruegel the Elder, *Peasant Wedding*, about 1565

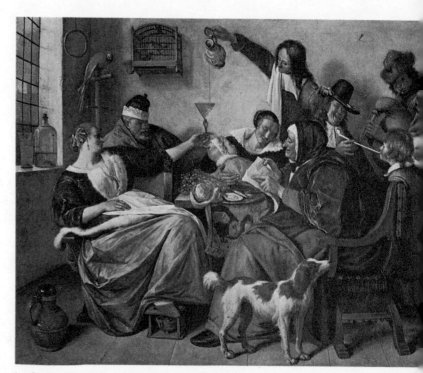

Jan Steen, *Merry Company*, about 1663

Jan Vermeer, *The Artist in His Studio*, about 167

58

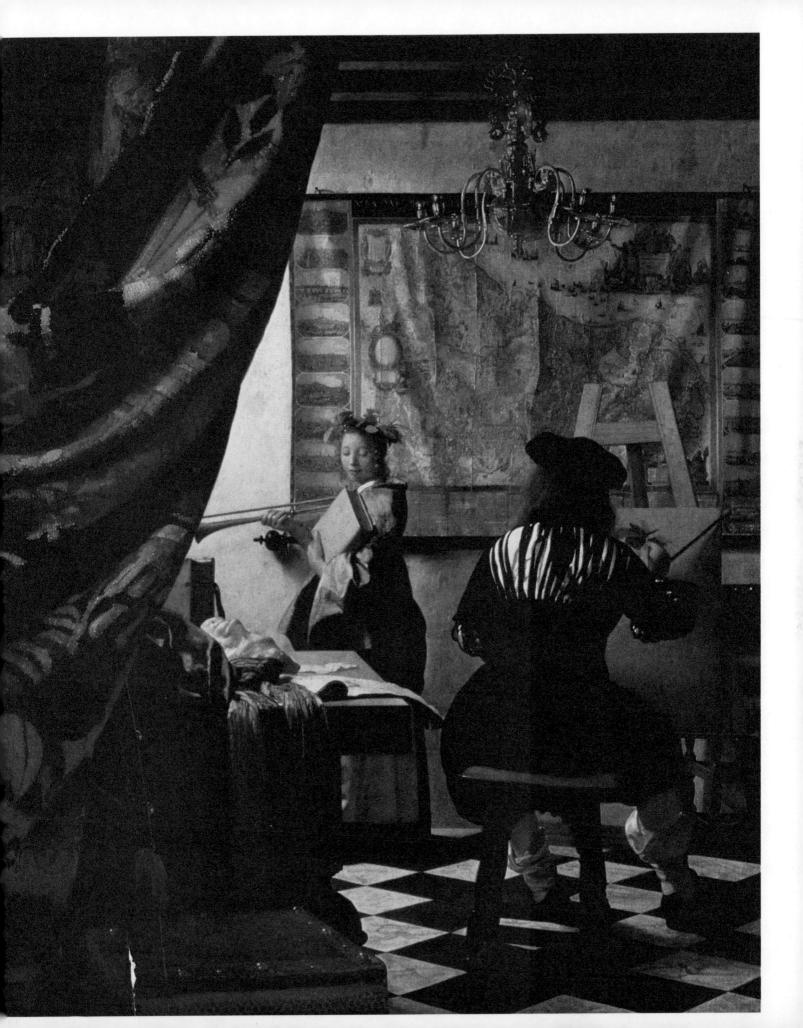

The Flemish painter **Peter Paul Rubens** was a great master of the baroque style. But he was much more than that. He was an international diplomat, a post in which his mastery of a number of languages and his self-assured courtly manner served him well. His friendship as well as his services were esteemed by princes of several lands, once and for all demolishing the belief that an artist was merely a skilled craftsman. His energy was boundless and his work in such demand that he developed what has been called a "factory" of helpers. Some 2,000 paintings have been attributed to his studio. His self-portrait with his beautiful wife, Isabella Brandt, shows the artist as a relatively young man.

Hans Holbein the Younger was a German-born artist who worked in Switzerland and, most importantly, in England, where he painted portraits of King Henry VIII in all his finery. He was the good friend of such distinguished men as Sir Thomas More. Like Rubens', his output was incessant and huge. He was internationally famous and was considered the most celebrated German artist of his time.

Antoon (later Sir Anthony) **van Dyck** studied under Rubens and as a young man won that master's highest praise. He was charming socially, highly intellectual, and confident enough of his stature as an artist to become somewhat arrogant. During his visit to Italy the Romans called him "the knightly painter." When Charles I of England became king, he summoned Van Dyck to London to grace the court there with his talents and his social presence. (England had no equally famous artist of its own.) Van Dyck painted many portraits of the king and his family and was showered with honors and lavish gifts, which included a knighthood, a townhouse with six servants, a summer residence, and a handsome pension.

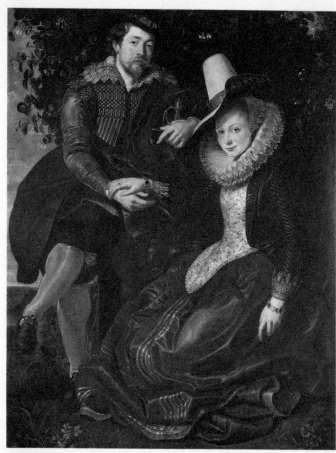

Peter Paul Rubens, *Self-Portrait with Isabella Brandt*, about 1610

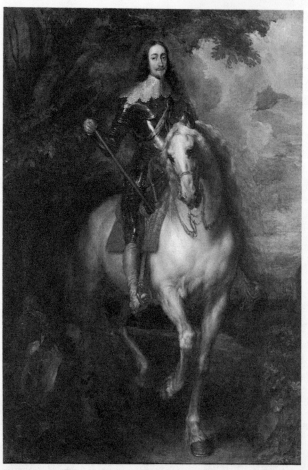

Hans Holbein the Younger, *Henry VIII,* 1540

Anthony van Dyck, *Charles I of England,* 1635

ANNO · ETATIS ·   · SVÆ · XLIX ·

As is the case in a number of his other portraits, **Frans Hals's** *Yonker Ramp and His Sweetheart* seems to be a completely spontaneous painting. It is as though the artist, with quick, slashing brushstrokes, has instantly—almost with snapshot speed—caught happy laughter, dancing eyes, and joyful gestures and fixed them forever on his canvas. Actually Hals created his effects with painstaking care. He is usually associated with such carefree and jovial characters as he pictured here. By reputation he was just such a hearty drinker himself. After considerable success, in his last years Hals became a public charge.

Rembrandt van Rijn was the greatest of all Dutch painters. His output was enormous and he had a strong influence on the course of European painting. One of Rembrandt's first important commissions for a group of portraits was *The Anatomy Lesson of Dr. Tulp.* Tulp stands at the right, lifting a red strand of muscle from a corpse with a scalpel. His observers are grouped before him, watching the demonstration more or less attentively. All the standing figures emerge from the darkness in a mysterious golden light. (This contrast of light and dark is called chiaroscuro.) Each individual portrait is a separate masterpiece, but the dramatic intensity of the whole scene has rarely been surpassed in any painting.

Jacob van Ruisdael, a younger contemporary of Rembrandt's, was the most talented of the large number of Dutch landscapists and an artist of great originality. His views of the flat Dutch countryside—with its canals, rivers, and windmills—are strictly true to nature. He painted thousands of them.

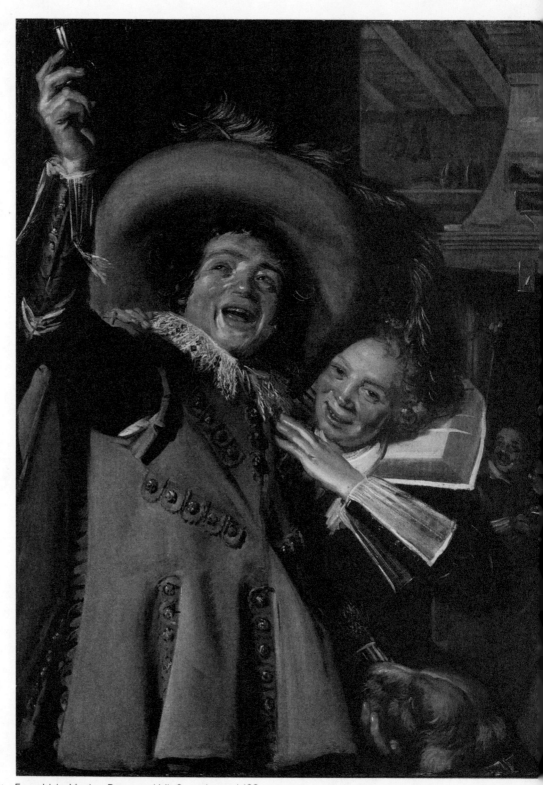

Frans Hals, *Yonker Ramp and His Sweetheart,* 1623

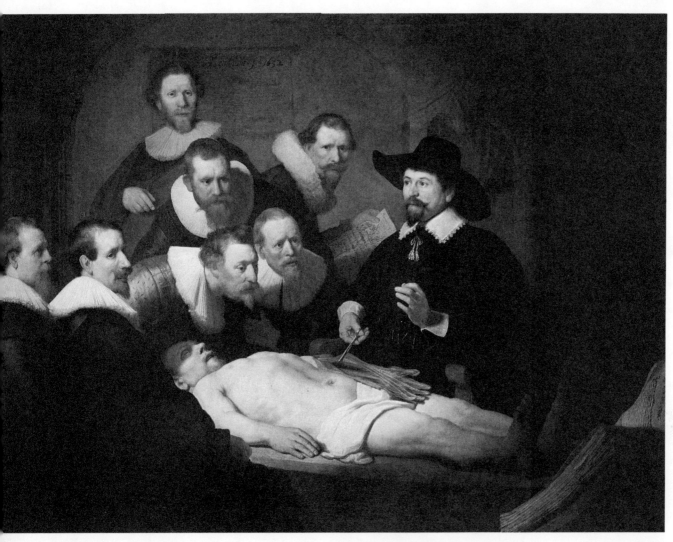

Rembrandt van Rijn, *The Anatomy Lesson of Dr. Tulp*, 1632

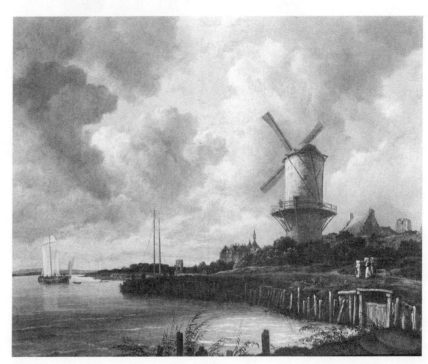

Jacob van Ruisdael,
The Mill at Wijk, Near Duurstede, 1667

Diego Velázquez spent thirty-seven years of his life as court painter to the monarchs of Spain. King Philip IV also chose him as a close friend. When Velázquez died, Philip wrote "I am crushed" in a memorandum. By that time the artist had proved himself the finest painter in Spanish history—one of the best in *all* history. *Maids of Honor* is one of his most famous works. Here he portrayed the little princess Margarita among her playmates and maids of honor. The artist is working on a huge canvas. A mirror on the wall reflects the faces of the king and queen. Like Vermeer and Caravaggio, Velázquez was fascinated with light. Here he played it on his subjects in different ways to illuminate their separate roles in the scene.

Louis le Nain and his brothers, Antoine and Mathieu, are remembered for their matter-of-fact, somewhat primitive paintings of 17th-century French peasant life, unusual subjects in the art of that time.

El Greco's real name was Domenico Theotocopoulos. He was born in Greece, went to Venice (where he may have studied with Titian), then on to Rome, and finally in 1576 to Spain where he lived out his days. There he was always considered an eccentric foreigner. His highly original works—with their strangely distorted, almost weightless figures and unreal colors—fascinated some and repelled others. For a time he prospered, then lost favor. Thereafter his work was almost neglected until our own day, when his fame is even greater than it was during his lifetime.

Nicolas Poussin was the earliest French painter to win international fame. He spent much of his life in Rome. There he was exposed to the classical tradition of art, which inspired him with its orderliness and its references to an ancient past. He is well remembered for his ideal landscapes, such as this one showing the remains of the great Athenian general Phocion being carried to their final resting place in a rustic scene with a background of classical buildings.

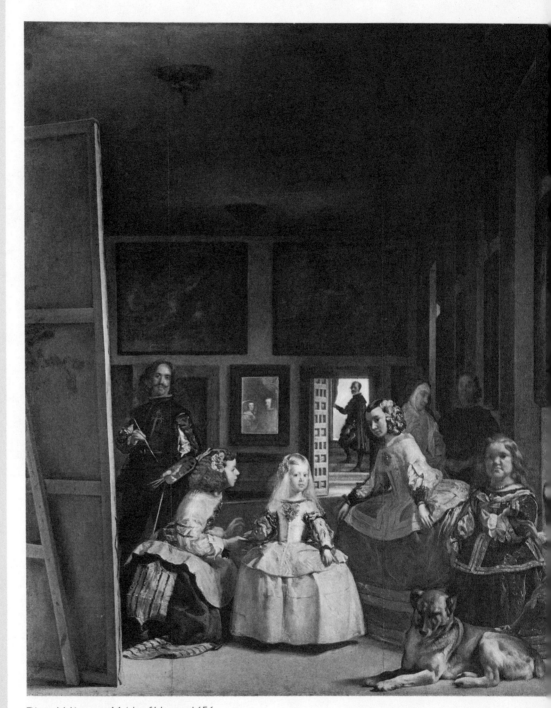

Diego Velázquez, *Maids of Honor*, 1656

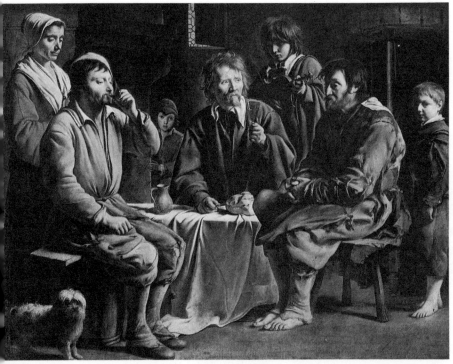

Louis le Nain, *Peasant Meal,* 1642

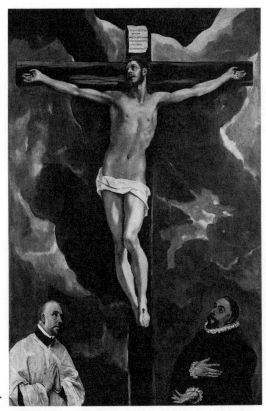

El Greco, *Christ Crucified with Two Donors,*
about 1590–1600 ▶

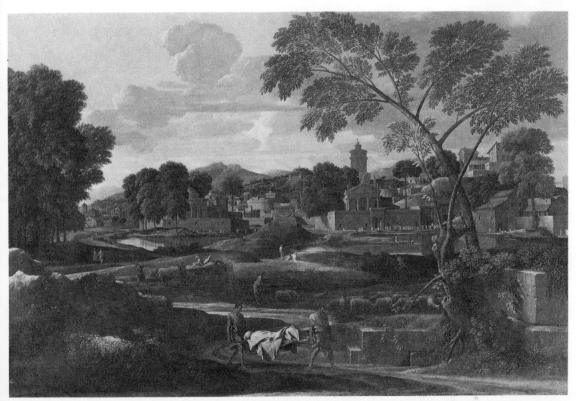

Nicolas Poussin, *Landscape with the
Burial of Phocion,* 1648

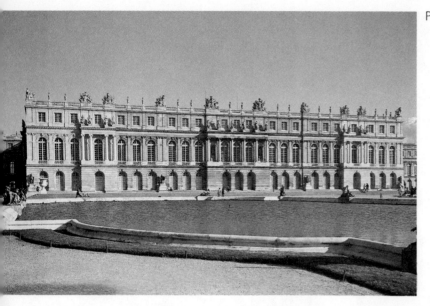

THE 18th AND 19th CENTURIES

As we have seen earlier in this book, the mainstreams of art have changed their course only gradually throughout much of history. For relatively long periods of time, old, established styles gave way to new ones grudgingly. But in the 18th and 19th centuries, the leading styles in art tended to change at an increasingly rapid pace. And so did practically everything else that affected the lives of people.

The 18th century has been called the Age of Enlightenment or the Age of Reason. Wise men of that time believed that humankind would find freedom and happiness through the exercise of reason in all matters. By fearlessly questioning the authority and conventions that had for so long governed their lives, people would throw off the burden of old, worn-out traditions that hindered their progress toward a brighter future.

It was an age of political and social revolutions that altered the outlook of large numbers of people. First there was the American Revolution of 1776. This was quickly followed by the French Revolution of 1789. Soon afterward came the world-shaking developments brought about by Napoleon's victories—and defeats. In the aftermath of those great disturbances, the people in several European countries, striving for greater freedom, rebelled against their rulers. So did the people of Mexico and other Latin American countries.

At the same time the Industrial Revolution was transforming the daily lives of untold numbers of people. Newly invented power-driven machinery was relieving working people from labors that had been drudgingly performed by human muscle for all the years of past history. However, it also eliminated many of their jobs altogether. For the unemployed and for the underpaid factory workers the new machinery was a very doubtful blessing. The more fortunate of the factory owners, however, became newly rich. One consequence of their prosperity was that the arts came to serve a growing public of varied and changing tastes.

It was in this climate of thought and activity that leadership in the arts passed from Italy to France. Also during this period, art made an early brave showing in America, then went on to establish a worthy tradition of its own in this freest of lands. When the leadership again changed hands, it passed from France to America in the present century.

The series of radical changes that would overtake the arts started gradually. The monumental grandeur of baroque art lingered on into the early 18th century before giving way to more informal styles.

Even kings and their ladies at times found the splendid formality of their palaces overwhelming. More modest homes were designed for them to enhance comfort, convenience, and privacy. This fashion spread to people of lesser rank.

As rooms became smaller and more intimate, paintings in turn became smaller. They were meant to be hung in drawing rooms, dining rooms, parlors, and bedrooms rather than for display on palace walls.

A greater variety of subject matter was called for, often revealing conflicting, or at least widely divergent, points of view. On one hand, French painting pictured the carefree life in courtly circles in the decades leading up to the revolution. In sharp contrast, other artists represented the more sober realities of daily life among more modest folk, even including the dishes from which they ate and drank.

As its prosperity increased, the landed gentry in England had itself portrayed quietly enjoying life on its well-kept countryseats while Hogarth, the first truly English artist, showed the more seamy side of society.

Italian artists painted vistas of their native land, which had become a favorite resort for wealthy British tourists.

In America well-to-do colonists commissioned likenesses of themselves in the manner of the great British portraitists. The demand was large enough to encourage a number of European artists to try their luck in the New World.

In the 19th century, following the American and French revolutions, France led the art world through a succession of new developments. Paris was so importantly the center of influence that the standards set there were adopted internationally. Artists of the world went to school in France.

At the peak of his tumultuous career Napoleon Bonaparte saw himself as a successor of the great empire builders of ancient Rome. He had the artist Jacques-Louis David portray him in this role. This sparked a revival of interest in the classical past.

Excavations of long-forgotten Roman sites revealed new evidence of how the ancients lived, the furniture they used, and the clothes they wore. This in turn renewed interest in the surviving ruins from antiquity and sparked a revival of interest in the classical past to which David referred in his paintings. David, as court painter, was so busy and had to employ so many assistants that his shop amounted to an official school of art. The classical revival style quickly spread all over Europe and on to the United States.

Before that fashion subsided (it never really died out) art entered a new phase: the Romantic movement. The orderly and rigid conventions of the classical school gave way to a freer style of painting with which the individual artist expressed his emotions. Often his subjects were scenes of dramatic action (sometimes inspired by Romantic literature of the period), exotic places, or moody landscapes. The Romantic movement lingered on as still other fashions took the limelight.

Styles may come and go but most artists, whatever their particular approach to painting, have tried to show the real world in ways that made their subjects easily recognizable. The subjects of the Romantics were recognizable, but they tended to draw the mind away from the humdrum realities of daily living. About 1850 there was a renewed interest in bringing art back to earth. Some artists chose to reveal the commonplace facts of life without disguising the harsh realities that industrial progress left untouched, such as sweating peasants at work in their fields.

In America, with the wealth available from a booming economy, painting became a popular art during the middle decades of the 19th century. These years saw the beginnings of a significant tradition in landscape painting. In lyrical pictures of the hills and lakes, the valleys and rivers of their still semi-wild continent, artists portrayed the beauty and grandeur of the American land. In those optimistic years other artists were taking a close look at the common man in his rural village and farm, confidently and independently going about his business.

One of the very important developments in painting came with the invention of photography. Many artists concluded that it was pointless to try and match the utter realism of the camera. They came to believe that it was more important to give colorful impressions of what they saw through their sensitive eyes. This "impressionistic" view of the world brought about a violent but bloodless revolution in art that shocked many and attracted others who saw in it a new avenue of creativity. What we call modern art had been born. With many twists and turns that revolution continues, as we will see in the next chapter.

Jean-Baptiste-Siméon Chardin was born in 1699 and lived for eighty years. His still lifes and candid pictures of simple people going about their domestic routines or enjoying their modest pleasures are all straightforward and without mawkish sentiment. As in his *Young Lady with a Shuttlecock*, his aim was to reveal the goodness and truth in everyday life.

Jean-Antoine Watteau died of tuberculosis in 1721 when he was just 37 years old. He was the first important French artist to break away from the grandeur of the baroque style practiced during the reign of the Sun King, Louis XIV, and to introduce the lighter, less formal painting that became typical of French art in the 18th century. He reduced painting to a human scale. His work was very distinctive. It has a dreamlike quality, tinged with a melancholy and languor that may have been caused by his fatal illness.

Louis XIV had banned the Italian actors who had been so popular in France, but their traditions were continued by French actors in whom Watteau found favorite subjects for his work. He often used his friends as models, dressing them in theatrical costumes kept in his studio, as in his portrait of his friend Gilles. Even when he pictured his comedians and elegantly dressed people partying in real parks, Watteau leaves us with a feeling that happiness, like a dream, is fleeting.

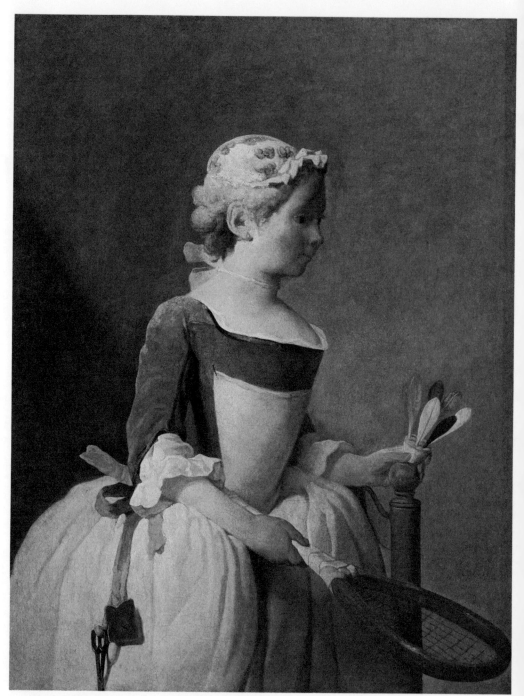

Jean-Baptiste-Siméon Chardin, *Young Lady with a Shuttlecock*, 1737

Jean-Antoine Watteau, *Gilles*, about 1718–20 ▶

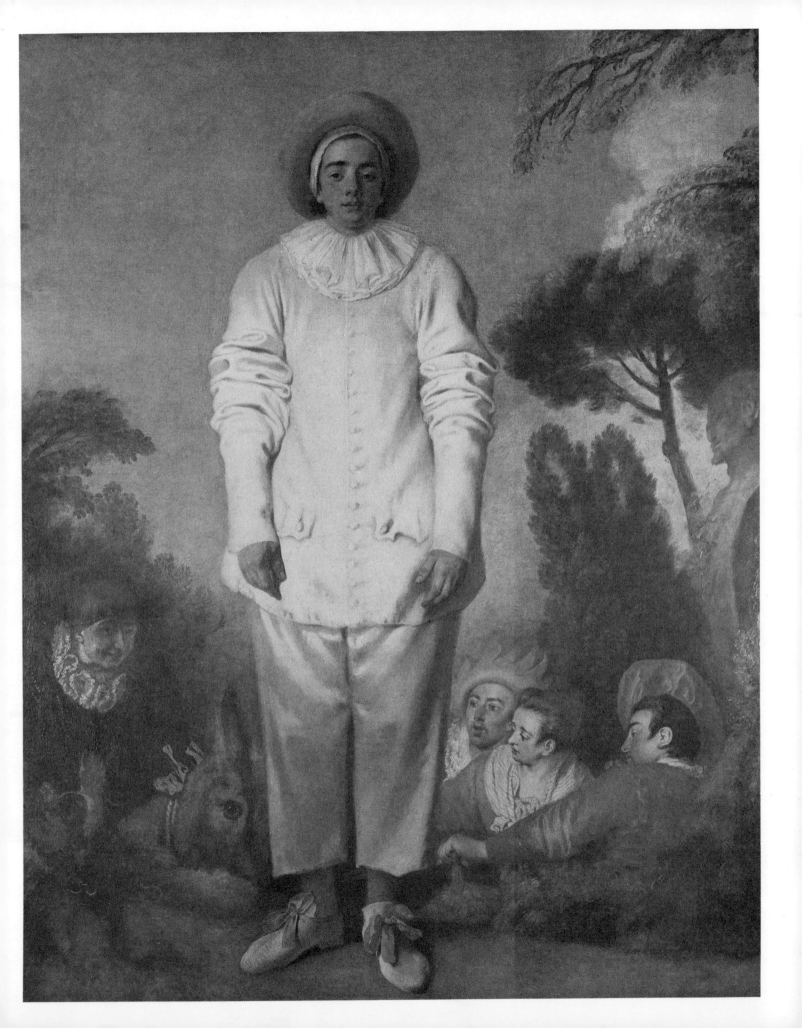

William Hogarth was a middle-class Englishman who found his universe in 18th-century London. He is best remembered for several series of engravings, for the most part copies of his paintings, in which he ridiculed the outlandish behavior of Britain's upper class. In doing this, he was probably the first artist to use his talent as a weapon of social criticism and was the first, as well, to direct his work to a large, unsophisticated public. Naturally his pictures did not appeal to the aristocracy, an artist's main source of patronage at the time. He was a fine portraitist and his human sympathies are clearly shown in *Shrimp Girl,* where he pictured this ordinary person with a candid smile and cheeks reddened by the sea winds.

Jean-Honoré Fragonard was the last of the great French artists who worked before the French Revolution. His paintings pictured the sensual delights of life. *Bathers* was typical of Fragonard's style, which appealed to the high-living French upper class in which he himself moved with zest. He was one of the earliest French artists to sell his pictures directly from his studio instead of putting them on public exhibition.

The 18th-century English artist **Thomas Gainsborough** never left England. He was both a landscapist and a portraitist and both of these aspects of his art are combined in *Conversation in a Park.* The seated couple are quite as important as the setting in which the artist pictured them. The country squire and his wife apparently belong to this pleasant land, as it in turn belongs to them.

One of the greatest French portraitists was the sculptor **Jean-Antoine Houdon.** His living likeness of Voltaire strongly suggests the searching intelligence, the biting wit, and the cynical insights of this great champion of wisdom.

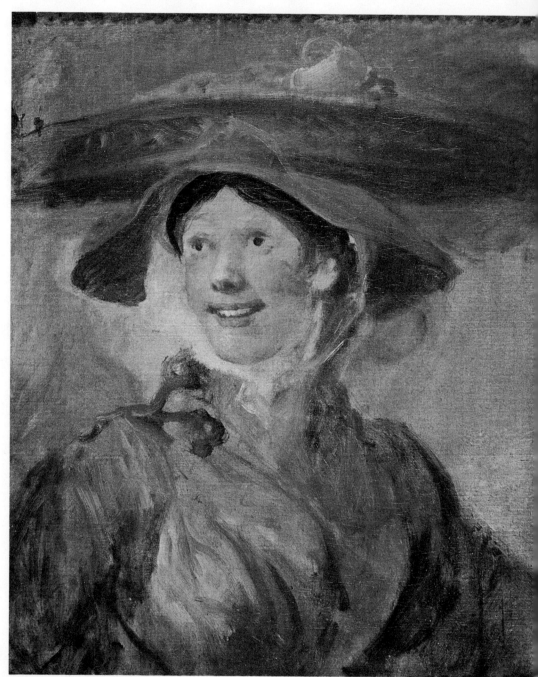

William Hogarth, *Shrimp Girl,* 1740

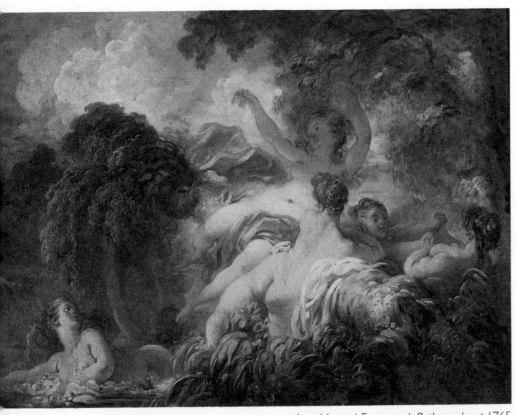

Jean-Honoré Fragonard, *Bathers*, about 1765

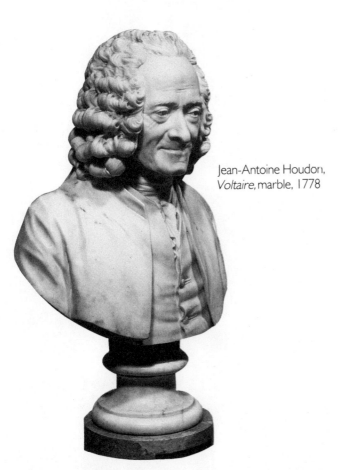

Jean-Antoine Houdon,
Voltaire, marble, 1778

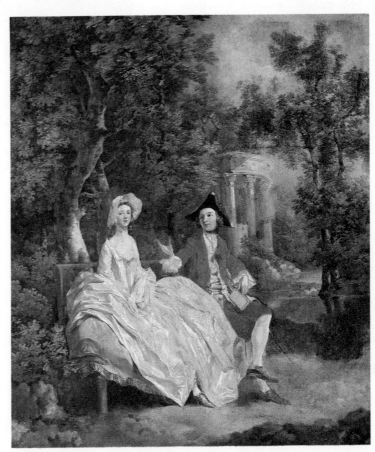

Thomas Gainsborough, *Conversation in a Park*, about 1746–47

Canaletto's painting of the great Venetian church Santa Maria della Salute on the Grand Canal is typical of the many views of the city turned out by this popular Italian artist. In the 18th century Venice was a high point in the grand tours of Europe made by fashionable and prosperous English people. The English travelers were very fond of this painter and brought his paintings home with them. There was hardly a great house in England that did not have one or more Canalettos. The Duke of Bedford once purchased two dozen of them in a single transaction. When wars on the Continent interrupted international travel, Canaletto moved to England, which continued to be the major market for his works.

Francisco Goya was one of the truly great Spanish artists. He was active in the late 1700s and early 1800s. He is well remembered for the complete candor of his portraits—even those of the Spanish royal family, whom he saw and painted as extremely unattractive people. (Goya was the official painter of the king.) He found a much more attractive subject in the seductive Duchess of Alba, whose lover he became. Two of his portraits of her reclining on a couch, one fully clothed and one in the nude (as here), are among his most celebrated paintings. In midlife he lost his hearing. He continued to paint and to make extraordinary prints for almost forty more years. Some of his other important works reveal a profound disillusionment with humankind.

When it was first exhibited in Rome in the late 1700s, **Jacques-Louis David's** *Oath of the Horatii* created a sensation. The artist pictured three young Roman warriors receiving their swords from their father and pledging to return from battle victorious or dead on their shields. By using classical settings for his paintings, David helped revive a vision of the heroic grandeur of the ancient Roman republic. That classical revival affected the design of clothing, furniture, and architecture as well as styles in painting for a number of years.

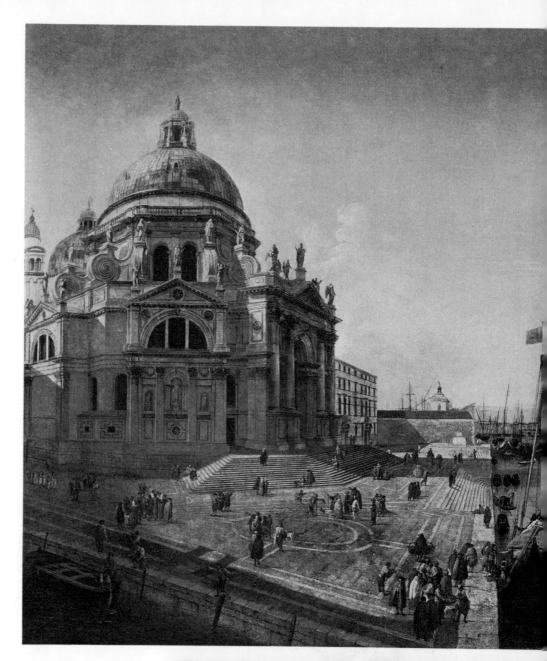

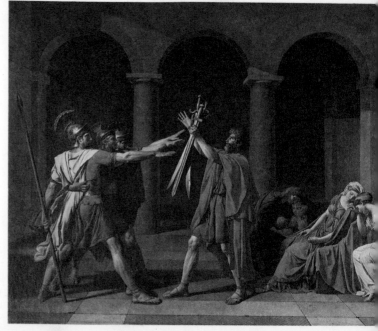

Jacques-Louis David,
The Oath of the Horatii, 1784

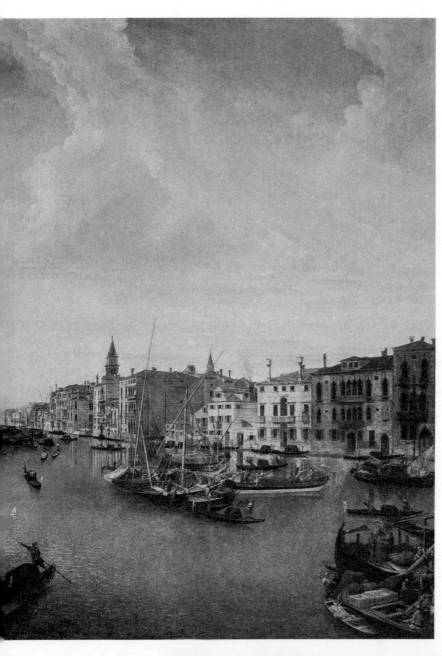

Canaletto, *Santa Maria della Salute and the Grand Canal,* 1730

Francisco Goya,
The Naked Maja, about 1795–97

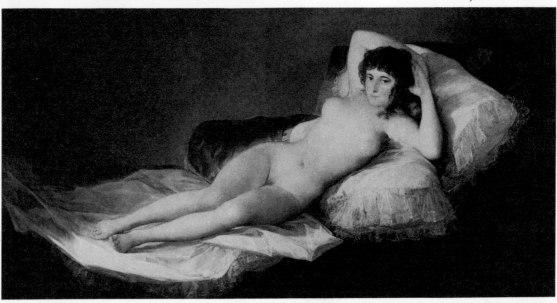

The Bostonian **John Singleton Copley** was a largely self-taught artist. He was also the finest painter in colonial America. The likenesses he made of his countrymen were better paintings than he had ever seen. His portrait of Paul Revere, painted a few years before the outbreak of the American Revolution, shows that patriot and craftsman in his work clothes at his workbench with the tools of his trade, holding a silver teapot he was in the course of making. A few years later Copley went to England to find greater opportunities to practice his art. He never returned to his homeland.

In 1792, after several years of study and portrait painting in England and Ireland, **Gilbert Stuart,** a native Rhode Islander, returned to America with the intention of painting a portrait of George Washington. This he did several times over. In doing so, he created a standard image of the father of this country that has been endlessly reproduced ever since. If Washington ever returned to earth, he would have to resemble Stuart's portraits to be recognized.

Charles Willson Peale was at one time or another an artist, a saddler, a soldier, an author, a naturalist, an inventor, a silversmith, an engraver, a museum director, and an upholsterer—among still other things. In 1795 he painted a remarkable life-size double portrait of two of his sons (artists also) on a winding staircase. It is known as the *Staircase Group.* It was so lifelike that, the story goes, George Washington bowed politely to the painted figures as he passed, thinking them living persons.

A detail from a painting by **Samuel F. B. Morse,** inventor of the telegraph as well as an artist, shows Congress Hall, or the old House of Representatives, at lamplighting time. The entire painting includes eighty-odd miniature portraits. This, with its solemn, dramatic lighting and its skilled handling of perspective, makes it a remarkable job of accurate pictorial reporting. However, it aroused little public interest at the time.

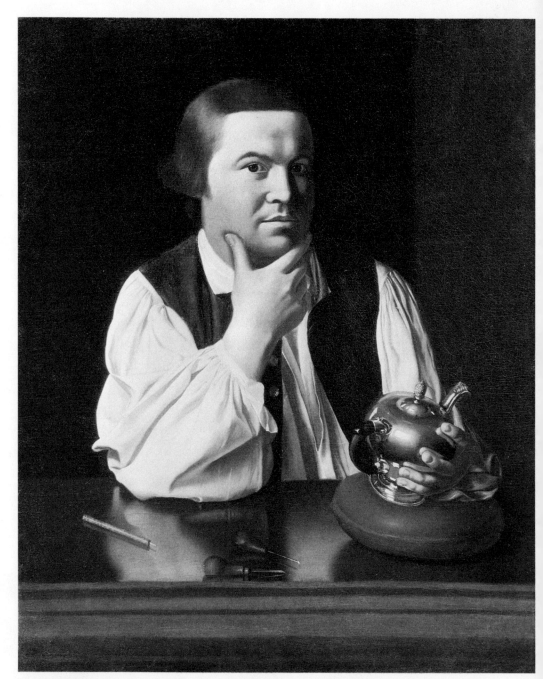

John Singleton Copley, *Paul Revere,* about 1768–70

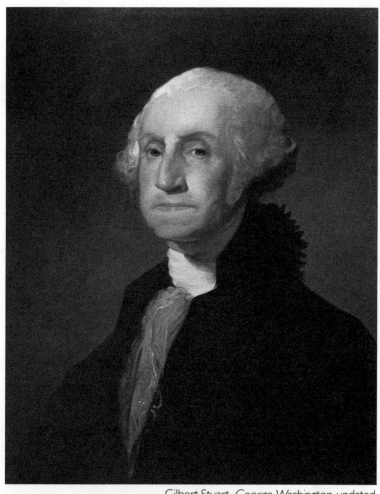

Gilbert Stuart, *George Washington*, undated

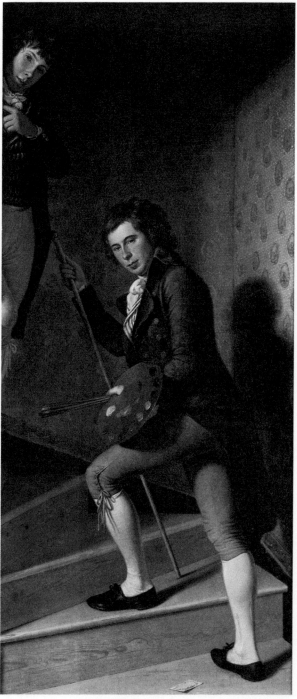

Charles Willson Peale, *Staircase Group*, 1795

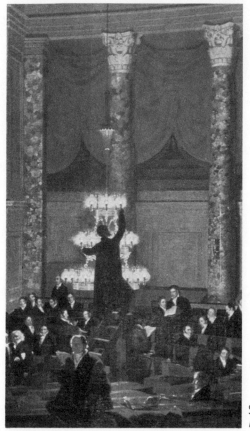

Samuel F. B. Morse, *The Old House of Representatives* (detail), 1822

Raft of the "Medusa," painted when he was 27 years old, made **Théodore Géricault** famous. (He died five years later.) The *Medusa,* a French frigate, sank off the African coast in 1818 with the loss of many lives. One hundred forty-nine survivors crowded onto a makeshift raft. All but five of these died from thirst, starvation, exposure, suicide, and murder before a rescue ship arrived on the scene. This and others of Géricault's paintings are charged with melodrama and emotion. In his short life he became a leading figure in the new Romantic movement in art.

When **John Constable**'s *Haywain* was exhibited at the Paris Salon of 1824, it was awarded a gold medal—an extraordinary honor for an English artist to receive in France. Constable often painted landscapes out of doors instead of in a studio, an unusual thing to do at the time. With his rapid impressions of the natural world in all its true colors, Constable was the prophet of an English school of landscape painting. He painted what he saw as he saw it. The sky, the clouds, the trees, the meadows, and the streams were his real subjects. Almost everything else was incidental.

Constable's contemporary, **Joseph M. W. Turner**, used nature only as a starting point for his explosive and brilliant visions. His *Fighting "Téméraire"* pictures a famous old British warship being towed to its final berth, heading into a sunset scene of wind-whipped skies. It seems as though, with these dramatic effects, Nature is paying a fiery tribute to a tired but honorable veteran of many battles. In such landscapes the Romantic movement found skillful expression.

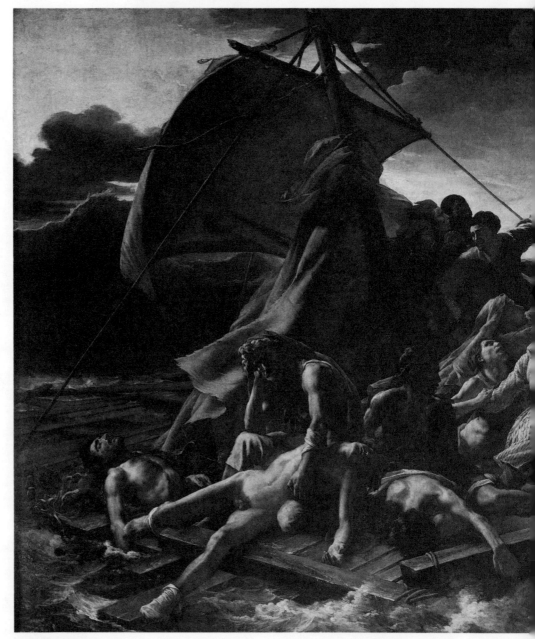

Théodore Géricault, *Raft of the "Medusa,"* 1818–19

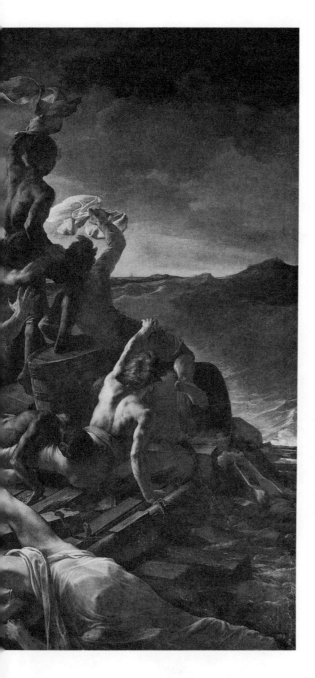

Joseph M. W. Turner, *The Fighting "Téméraire,"* 1838

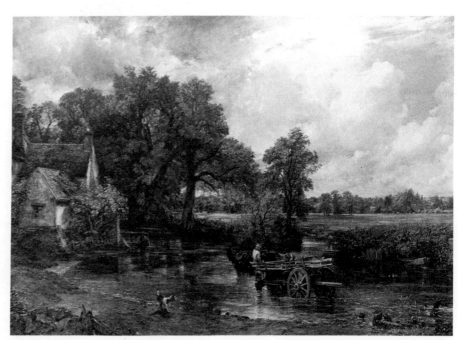

John Constable, *The Haywain,* 1821

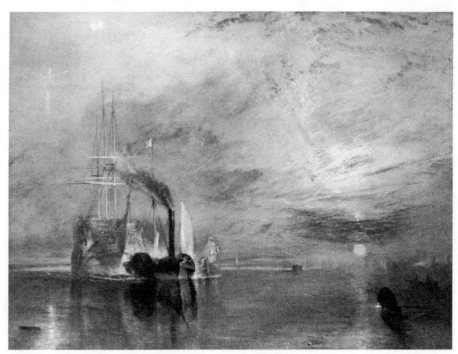

In 1849 the American artist **Asher Durand** painted a picture of his fellow artist Thomas Cole with the popular poet William Cullen Bryant. The two are shown standing on a rocky ledge of the Catskill Mountains near the Hudson River in New York. Bryant has his hat in his hand; Cole holds a book under his arm. Durand titled the painting *Kindred Spirits*. Durand and Cole were members of an unorganized group of artists, known as the Hudson River School, who pictured the newly perceived beauty and grandeur of their semi-wild continent as Bryant and others described it in their books. The Hudson River School produced the earliest American landscapes.

Fur Traders Descending the Missouri by **George Caleb Bingham** is one of the most appealing American paintings of the 19th century. He portrayed a French Canadian trapper with his half-breed son and their tethered pet floating downstream on a calm and misty day, bringing their precious furs to market. Whether the pet is a raccoon, a fox, or a cat has long been debated. Bingham grew up in the West. His paintings of life in the Missouri region were widely admired.

John James Audubon won international fame in the first half of the 19th century with his paintings of the birds of America. No artist before him had pictured birds with such scrupulous accuracy or shown them so faithfully in their natural habitats. His works gave Europe a fresh poetic vision that fired the imagination. "This beautiful and singular bird," he wrote of the roseate spoonbill, was "a regular article of trade with the hunters of St. Augustine, Florida."

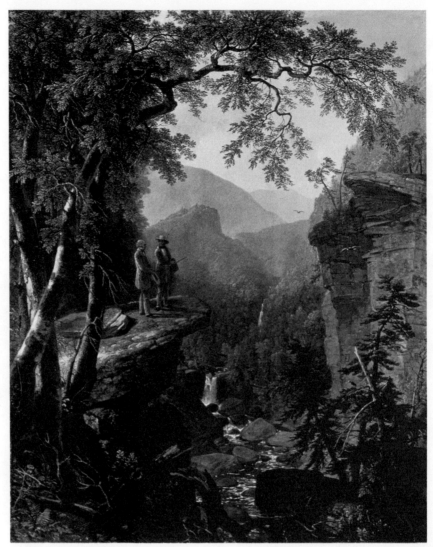

Asher Durand, *Kindred Spirits*, 1849

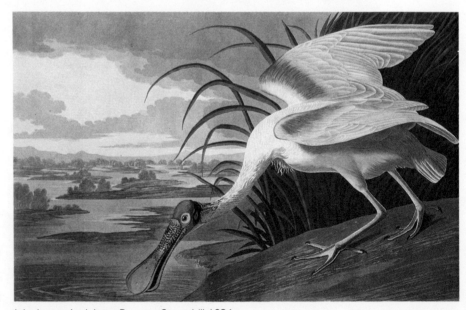

John James Audubon, *Roseate Spoonbill*, 1836

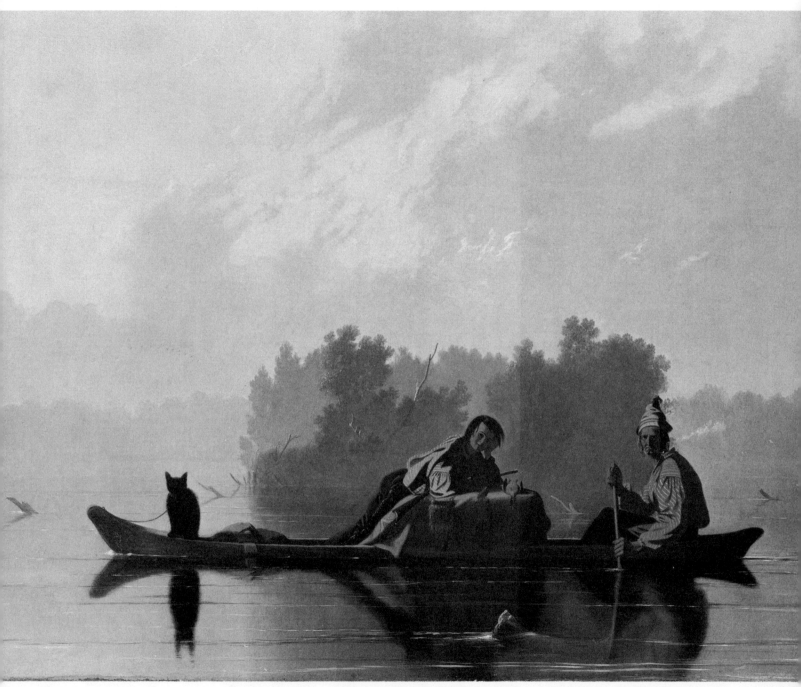

George Caleb Bingham, *Fur Traders Descending the Missouri*, 1845

The 19th-century French artist **Henri Fantin-Latour** is best remembered for his still-life paintings, which recall works by the Old Masters centuries earlier.

"Show me an angel," **Gustave Courbet** once remarked, "and I will paint one." This illustrates his belief that an artist should paint only pictures of the real world of his own day as truthfully as he can. Courbet was both acclaimed and condemned as an extreme Realist, and as a radical.

This detail from *The Painter's Studio* shows one of his models standing before a landscape on which the artist was then working, surrounded by his friends.

The American artist **William Michael Harnett** carried realism to the point where the objects on his canvases seem like real things rather than painted images. For a time, one of his works hung in a New York saloon where convivial customers were diverted and sometimes bewildered by the illusion of solid three-dimensional reality the artist had created.

Honoré Daumier was widely known for his thousands of cartoons, which were reproduced in French periodicals. Today he is considered one of the foremost French painters of his time. His *Crispin and Scapin* illustrates a scene from a play by the 17th-century playwright Molière. Like Courbet, Daumier too was a confirmed Realist, but in an entirely different fashion. To stress the true character of his subjects, he resorted to distortion, which made them resemble caricatures.

Jean François Millet referred to himself as the "peasant of peasants." His sentimental paintings of French farmers laboring in their fields won a wide audience in America a century ago.

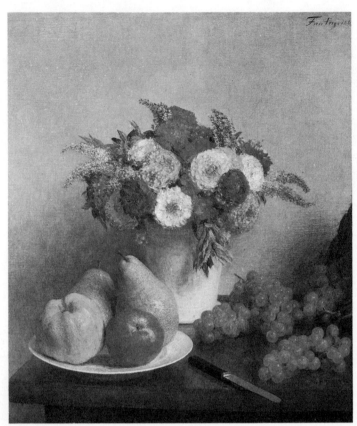

Henri Fantin-Latour, *Still Life*, 1869

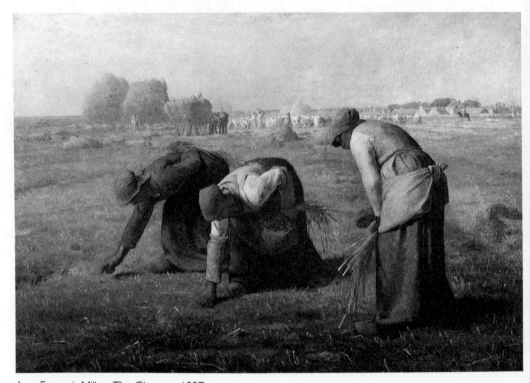

Jean François Millet, *The Gleaners*, 1857

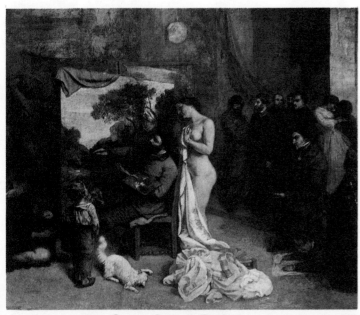

Gustave Courbet, *The Painter's Studio* (detail), 1855

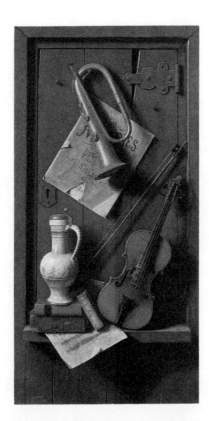

William Michael Harnett,
Old Models, about 1892

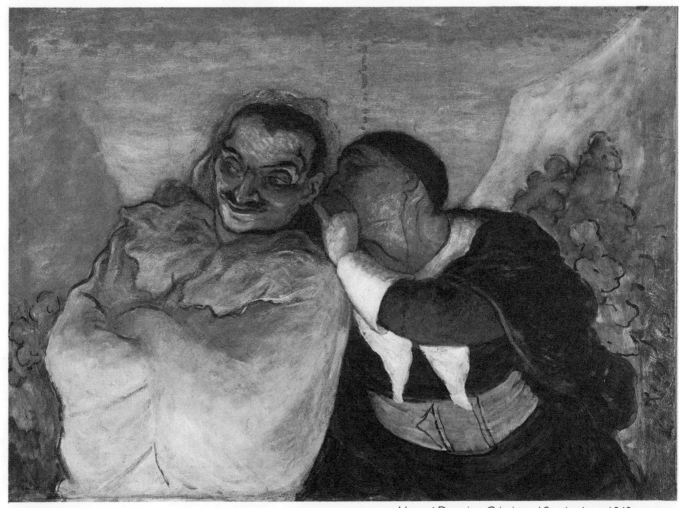

Honoré Daumier, *Crispin and Scapin*, about 1848

James A. M. Whistler was a 19th-century American artist who chose to live and work abroad. He was a celebrated wit, a socialite, a dandy, and a very good painter. With his work and his self-promoting antics he created a greater sensation in European art circles than any American artist had done since Benjamin West. He was the first American artist to belittle the importance of subject matter in painting. Art, he claimed, was for art's sake. He stressed formal, decorative patterns, which he differentiated from subject matter by labeling them Nocturnes, Symphonies, and Arrangements. Thus, the famous painting we know as *Whistler's Mother* he preferred to call *Arrangement in Black and Gray.*

For **Edouard Manet,** as for Whistler, the painting itself became more important than anything it might represent. Manet believed that this importance could be achieved primarily by color. This led the way to Impressionism. In 1863, when he applied these principles to his painting *Luncheon on the Grass,* critics greeted the result with ridicule. What, they asked, could a woman be doing sitting stark naked on the grass with two fully dressed men? To Manet this was an idle question. It was his intention to create—by whatever means—a memorable visual experience, which he did.

Whistler's younger American contemporary **John Singer Sargent** also lived much of his life overseas. Sargent's early paintings also caused a stir in art circles. Like Whistler before him, he moved from Paris to London, which became the center of his very successful career as a fashionable portraitist. To be "done" by Sargent for $5,000 and up was considered a distinction and a privilege. When he was painting for his own pleasure rather than for a client, he created watercolors of dazzling beauty.

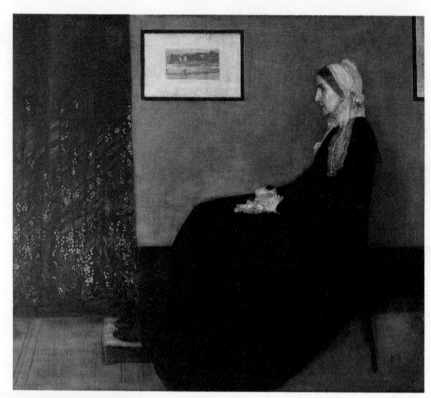

James A. M. Whistler, *Arrangement in Black and Gray: The Artist's Mother,* 1871

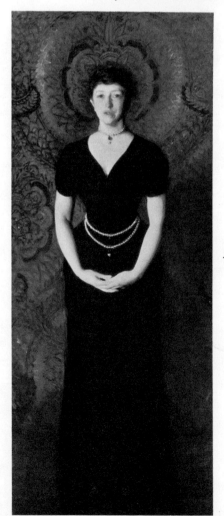

John Singer Sargent,
Portrait of Isabella Gardner, 1888

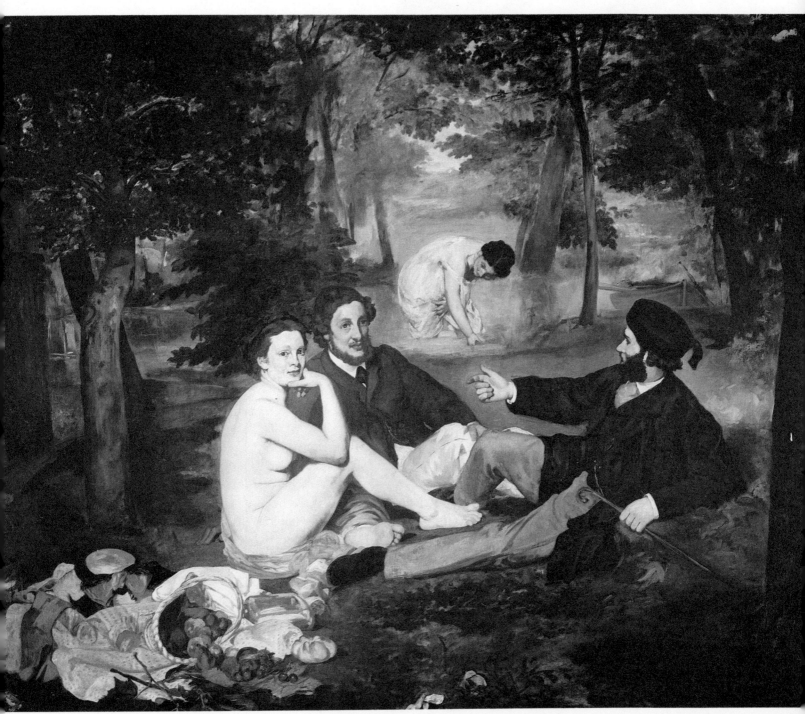

Edouard Manet, *Luncheon on the Grass,* 1863

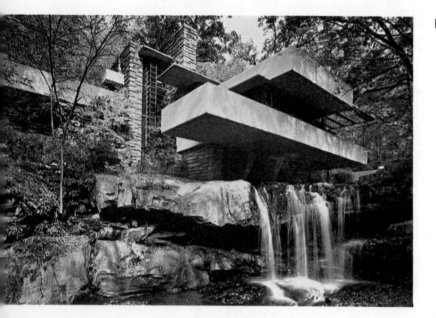

Frank Lloyd Wright, *Fallingwater*, 1936

ART OF
OUR TIMES

Art not only reflects the world we live in, it also helps explain that world to us. Looking back at the past, as we have been doing, we can see that our understanding of those times would be much less clear if we did not know the arts those times produced. For the arts often speak to us when histories remain dumb.

In recent decades, advances in technology have made today's world increasingly complex. To reflect the rapid changes that have taken place, artists have tried many new directions, methods, and materials. The 20th century has been an age of exploration in the art world as rich in discovery and adventure as was the 15th century, when men first found their way about the seven seas.

Modern technology has demolished barriers of time and distance at a bewildering rate. Through books such as this one we can become aware of more aspects of the world of art than were dreamed of by our grandparents and their parents. In the same way, modern artists can draw inspiration from the most remote and exotic cultures.

The term "modern art" is used here to include what has been created in the last hundred years or so. Some of it more or less faithfully follows traditional lines; some of it is extremely experimental.

It was in 1874 that a group of Impressionists in Paris held the first of their independent exhibitions. This was a challenge to the old guard of artists who had long controlled the official exhibitions of the day and who for the most part considered the Impressionists rebels in the cause of true art. The Impressionists did create the most profound revolution in painting since Giotto five centuries earlier. With his realism Giotto "opened a window on the world." With their innovations the Impressionists revealed new ways of looking at that world. They saw it as a world of shimmering brightness—a brightness made up of little dabs of color. The Impressionists applied such dots directly to their canvases instead of mixing the different colors on their palettes. The mixing was done in the eye of the beholder, as naturally happens when light reaches the retina. In this the artists had the advantage of recent scientific studies of light and newly developed synthetic pigments more brilliant than any previously available.

In their successful rebellion against the "authorities," the Impressionists helped to make two major points that have had a lasting influence on art. The first was that a painting can be more important in itself, as a pattern of colors and textures, than any story it may tell or whatever things it may represent. They also established the artist's right to paint however he or she wishes, without obeying traditional rules of perspective or representation. Taking advantage of these freedoms, artists in our century have experimented in many ways. The variety of styles that have evolved are given such names as fauvism, expressionism, surrealism, cubism, abstract expressionism, and so on.

To talk about all such "isms" can be more confusing than helpful. These are not watertight compartments into which we can always fit this or that particular painting. It is better to enjoy each painting in its particular style.

In many cases the modern artist has altered the natural appearance of the real world to form new harmonies of shapes and colors that tempt us to look again at that world and find unexpected pleasures and meanings in it. Other artists have eliminated all references to the real world in their work. They have used the flat surface of the canvas as a field for abstract patterns of their own invention, leaving us to find our own meaning or pleasure in those patterns.

All paintings are abstract to some degree. Every artist selects what he feels is most important from what he sees. This is true even of the realistic works of the modern American artist Andrew Wyeth, in which every blade of grass and grain of sand seem to be accounted for. "It's not what you put in but what you leave out that counts," he said.

In spite of all the violent forces loosed by various experiments in modern art, forces that tended to weaken ties with old, established traditions, a large number of influential painters have continued to represent the world about them more or less as it appears to the eye—or rather to the mind's eye, for each of us sees the world differently.

Men have always lived in what were for them modern times, although they were not as aware of that fact as we are today. We now expect changes in our world with every passing day. The 20th century has been a tumultuous period punctuated by two world wars and a number of other conflicts. In the course of those disturbing events important artists of many different countries have emigrated to the United States to practice their profession and to teach. It was in part thanks to the influx of foreign, notably German, scholars that the art school of New York University quickly developed into a major center of art studies. "Hitler is my best friend," remarked that school's director. "He shakes the tree and I collect the apples." About the time the United Nations headquarters was established in New York, that city became the art capital of the world. New York has been where the "action" is for the past several decades.

In science and technology there has been steady progress toward greater achievement. But the word "progress" does not apply to art. As we have seen, there has been a long succession of changes in styles and techniques as artists of each period in history have attempted to express the spirit of their own times. Artists continue to do so in our day. The better we understand this, the better we will realize that fine art is timeless in its appeal, no matter when it was created. The best art of our time will be different from the creations of the past, but not necessarily greater. We can hardly claim it will be an improvement on the works of the ancient Greeks or of the Renaissance masters.

In spite of all the material advances civilization has made, the mind and spirit of man have changed remarkably little over the thousands of years of human history. The best art of our times will take its place as a form of communication with all times.

Claude Monet's main goal in his painting was to capture effects of light out of doors. The quality of daylight constantly changes according to the hour, the weather, and the season. To demonstrate this, Monet painted some forty pictures of the facade of the Rouen Cathedral under as many different conditions. To seize a particular moment, he had little time to mix different colors on his palette before fixing them on a canvas. Rather, he rapidly applied pure colors in small, tightly spaced strokes and allowed the eye to blend them as it naturally blends our impressions of a colorful scene. He was one of the foremost proponents of the Impressionist movement.

Edgar Degas was associated with the Impressionists but he preferred to paint indoor scenes: the theater and intimate interiors. He will always be remembered for his drawings and paintings of ballet dancers, whom he also sculpted. In either medium, he usually showed the dancers in some momentary attitude of their practice or performance, as a quick snapshot might do.

Another 19th-century French painter, **Georges Seurat**, reached beyond Impressionism to find a new art that would be entirely his own. He devised a system, known as pointillism, of using tiny dots of pure color almost like a mosaic. The paint was applied according to scientific principles to create a deliberate design rather than to reproduce nature. He died in 1891 at the early age of 32, leaving this painting of a circus scene unfinished.

In his earlier works, **Auguste Renoir** also explored the shimmering effects of light and atmosphere. His painting of the Moulin de la Galette, a popular Paris dance hall, presents a gathering of spirited young people enjoying themselves in the open air. In the background the whirling figures become a patchwork of bright colors that almost dissolve in the sunlight.

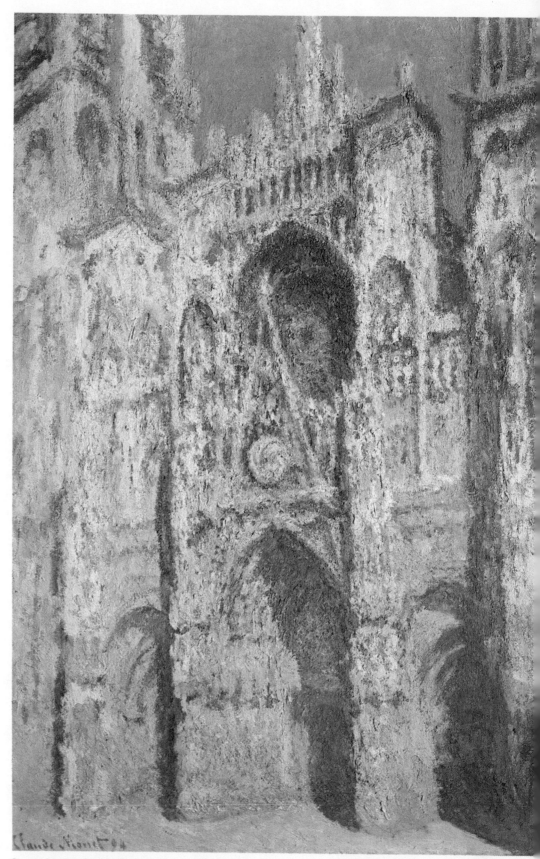

Claude Monet, *Rouen Cathedral,* about 1892–94

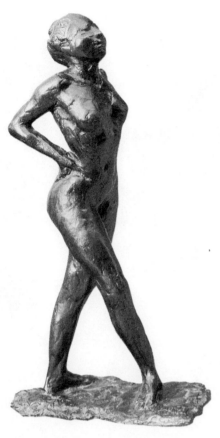

Edgar Degas, *Dancer at Rest,* 1882–95,
cast in bronze, 1919–21

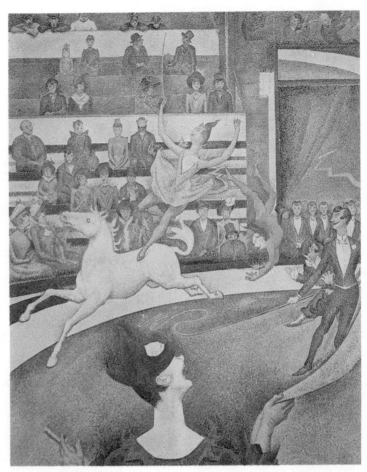

Georges Seurat, *The Circus,* 1891

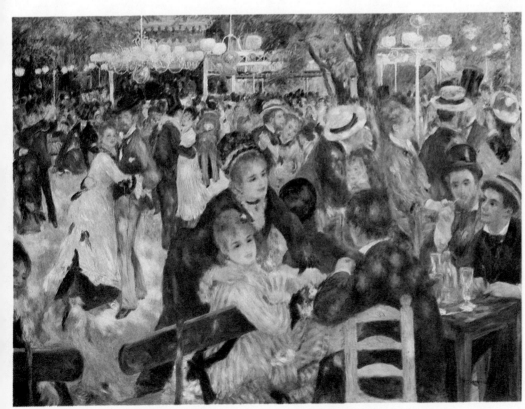

Auguste Renoir,
Moulin de la Galette, 1876

Mary Cassatt was the first important American woman artist. In Paris she became the only American artist to be associated with the central group of Impressionists. When Degas first saw one of her paintings, he exclaimed, "I would not have admitted that a woman could draw as well as that." Although she profited from her exposure to the works of Degas and of the Impressionists as a group, she copied none of them. She remained her own woman, an independent and talented spirit. She is known for her glowing depictions of women and their small children.

In the late 19th century the streets of Paris were filled with posters by **Henri de Toulouse-Lautrec.** In his hands the poster became a new art form. To serve its purpose the poster had to present a bold and colorful design combining type and image in a way that would quickly catch the eye of a passerby. Lautrec's announcement of the entertainer Aristide Bruant's appearance in his popular café, Les Ambassadeurs, does this perfectly.

Thomas Eakins was another great American Realist painter—too realistic for some. *The Gross Clinic* presents a dramatic moment in a surgical operation, when the surgeon, bloody scalpel in hand, turns from the body before him to address his audience. One of the listeners shields his eye from the scene before him. Some people were shocked by the gory details of the picture. An able, less squeamish critic called this "the most powerful and important painting by a 19th-century American artist."

In his own lifetime **Winslow Homer** was hailed as "the greatest American artist," "the most American painter," " the most intensely American painter of his time." In 1867 the *London Art Journal* reported that his works were "real. The artist paints what he has seen and known." There is no doubt that Homer had often seen and well knew scenes like the one he painted in *Breezing Up.* Here, as always, he reported his subject in his own honest and independent manner.

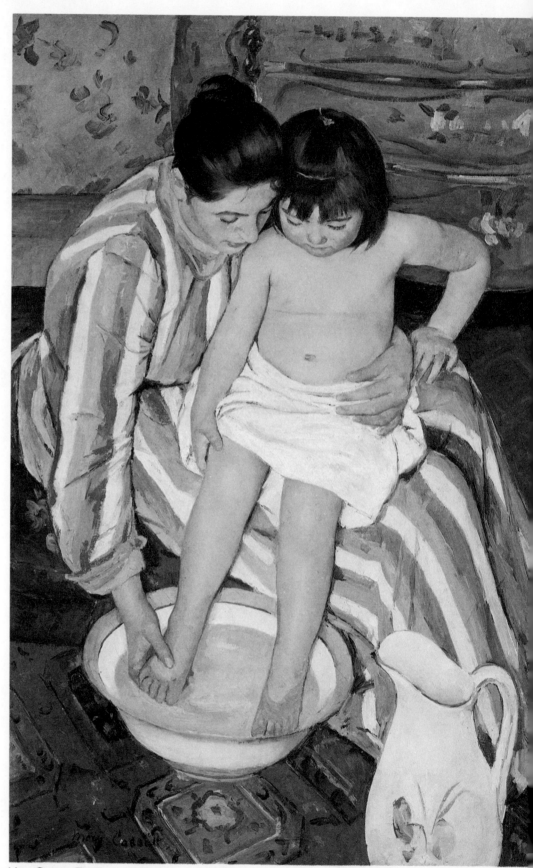

Mary Cassatt, *The Bath,* about 1892

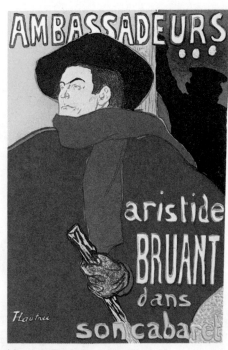

Henri de Toulouse-Lautrec,
Aristide Bruant at Les Ambassadeurs,
poster, 1892

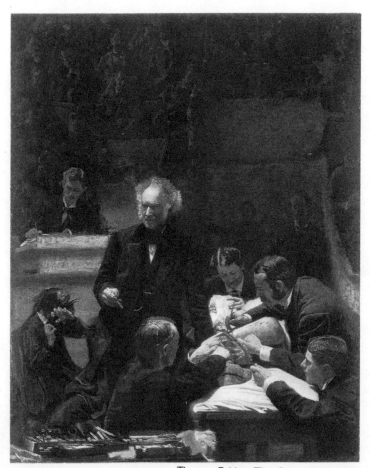

Thomas Eakins, *The Gross Clinic,* 1875

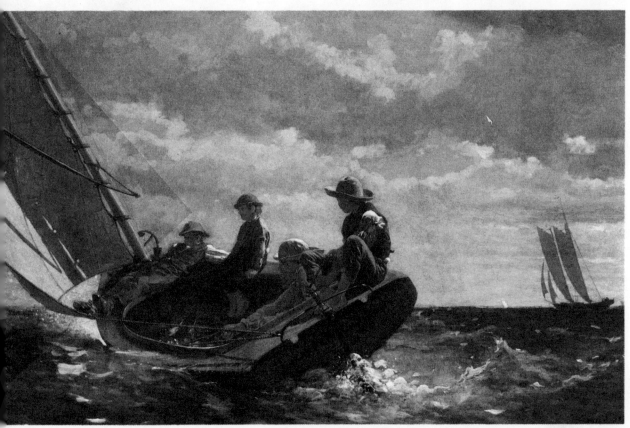

Winslow Homer, *Breezing Up,* 1876

The Dutch-born 19th-century artist **Vincent van Gogh** painted some of his best pictures in the south of France at a time when he was often emotionally unbalanced. His portrait of Dr. Paul Gachet, whose patient he became, shows how the artist expressed the intensity and violence of his vision with swirls and clusters of bright colors that seem almost to move on the canvas. A few months after finishing this painting, Van Gogh committed suicide at the age of 37.

The Norwegian painter and graphic artist **Edvard Munch** was dismayed by the human misery and loneliness he saw in the world around him. "I hear the screams in nature," he once wrote, a statement perfectly illustrated by the picture reproduced here. Like Van Gogh, Munch hoped with his explosive exaggeration of real forms to reach the inner truths rather than the appearances of the world we must live in. This was the beginning of a school of art called Expressionism.

Edouard Vuillard's typical paintings were of ordinary things which he placed in richly colored, quiet settings. His many interiors, such as *The Morning Meal*, shut out all sense of a world outside.

The French artist **Paul Gauguin** retreated to Tahiti to paint how and what he wanted in that distant, primitive, exotic world. We still tend to see that region as he chose to see it. But, as he noted, he was not a painter who worked from nature. "With me," he wrote, "everything happens in my wild imagination." He borrowed from many different sources, including Japanese prints, to create his own language of flat, brilliant colors arranged in decorative patterns. He gave a fresh direction to the development of modern art.

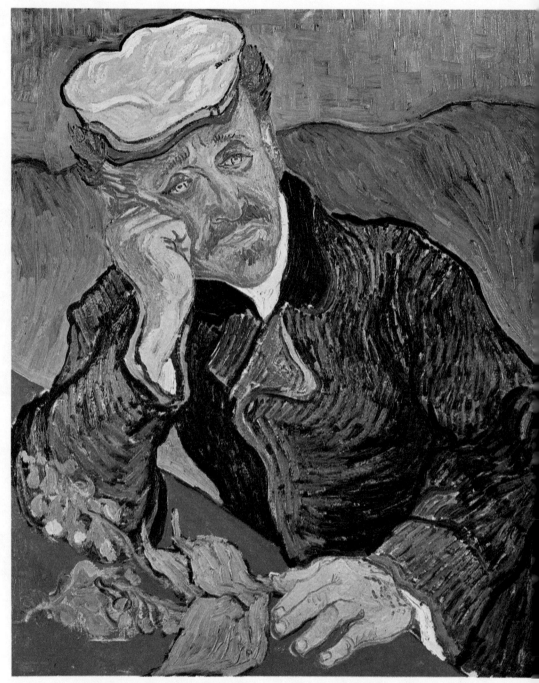

Vincent van Gogh, *Portrait of Dr. Gachet*, 1890

90

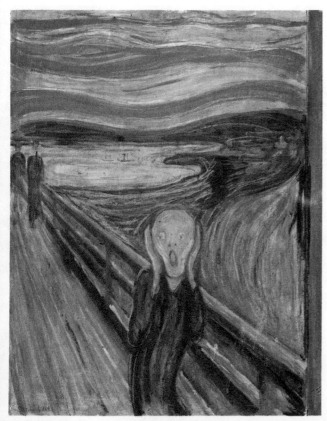

Edvard Munch, *The Scream*, 1893

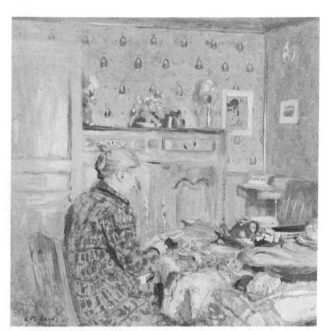

Edouard Vuillard, *The Morning Meal*, about 1900

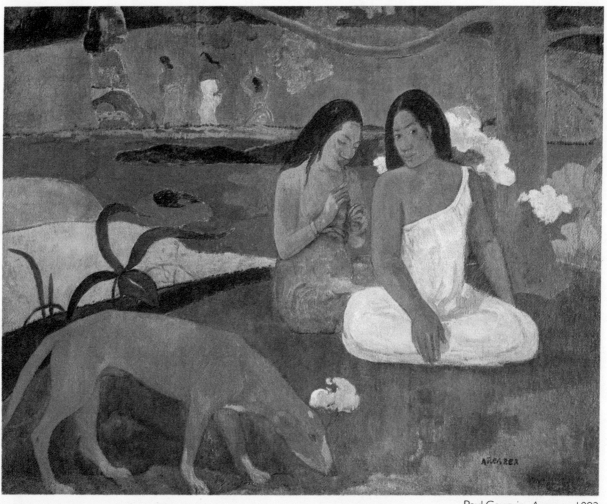

Paul Gauguin, *Arearea*, 1892

The famous Armory Show, staged in New York in 1913, was the most important art exhibition ever held in America. Here for the first time the American public at large was exposed to the most advanced art being produced in Europe, and to a great many it came as a shock. **Marcel Duchamp**'s *Nude Descending a Staircase* created the greatest furor. In this painting Duchamp translated the female form into a series of flashing shapes and lines suggesting rapid motion, as in a multiple-exposure photograph. One disapproving critic likened it to "an explosion in a shingle factory."

John Marin, one of the earliest modern artists in America, represented the rugged Maine coast, as he did the tall towers of Manhattan, in a lyrical pattern of form and color. He often used watercolor, which enabled him more quickly to record his momentary vision of the shore or the city.

The American painter **Maurice Prendergast** played a major part in organizing the Armory Show. His individual style, with its small flecks of bright color, was based on the impressionistic style in vogue in his student days in Paris. Early in this century one critic complained that the "spotty canvases" of Prendergast were "artistic tommy rot." When he finally won considerable success, he remarked, "I'm glad they've found out I'm not crazy, anyway."

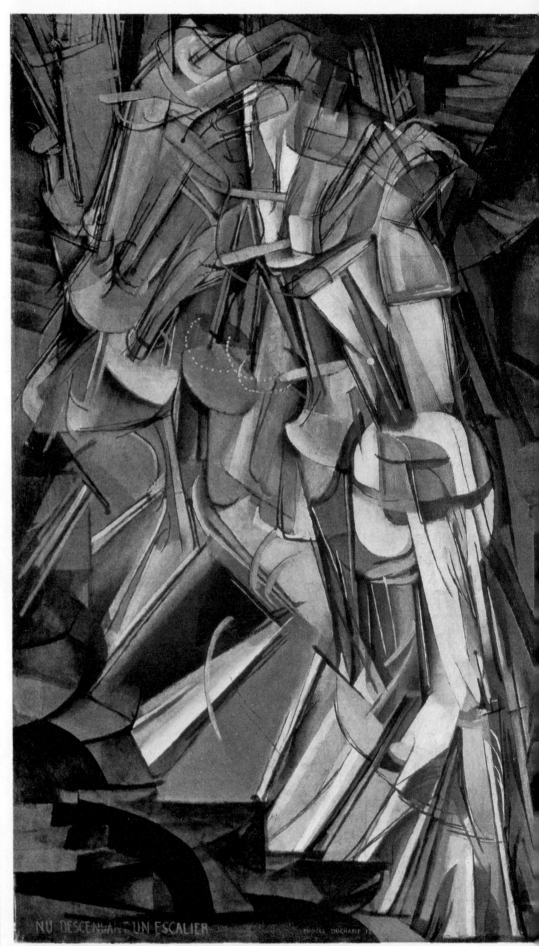

Marcel Duchamp, *Nude Descending a Staircase, No. 2,* 1912

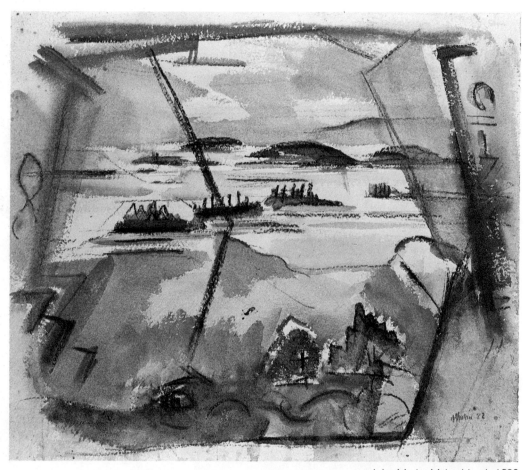

John Marin, *Maine Islands*, 1922

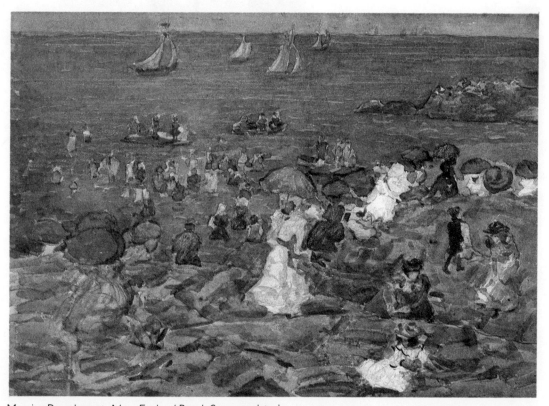

Maurice Prendergast, *New England Beach Scene*, undated

The Spanish-born artist **Pablo Picasso** probably worked in more different styles and media than any other artist in history. He also was probably the most influential artist of the 20th century. At one point in his career he was strongly drawn to primitive sculpture for his inspiration. This is evident in *Les Demoiselles d'Avignon,* finished in 1907, which was his first important composition. Before and after that painting, Picasso frequently changed his approach to art. His styles ranged from his early Blue Period to later ventures into fantasy and comic invention and included variations on the works of great masters.

Fernand Léger was an outstanding 20th-century French artist who is generally associated with a development known as "machine art." In some of his typical paintings, people and objects are reduced to machine-like forms. His style had a strong influence on modern decorators, designers, and commercial artists.

For a while another French artist, **Georges Braque,** collaborated so closely with Picasso that their works of that period can hardly be distinguished from one another. However, Braque was an important artist in his own right.

   Braque shared with Picasso a pioneering interest in cubism, an art style that relied for its effects on arrangements of planes and shapes rather than on color and perspective. The shapes were often transparent and placed on top of one another. No attempt was made to imitate nature. Braque also added unrelated elements, a technique known as collage.

Paul Cézanne has been called "the most revolutionary painter since the dawn of the Renaissance." He abandoned the idea of drawing realistically to create an illusion of reality. He sought instead to simplify the forms of nature into their basic shapes—planes, cubes, and cylinders—using color to create perspective and distorting natural forms to express their essence. He did this to perfection in a series of paintings of a mountain in southern France called Mont Sainte Victoire.

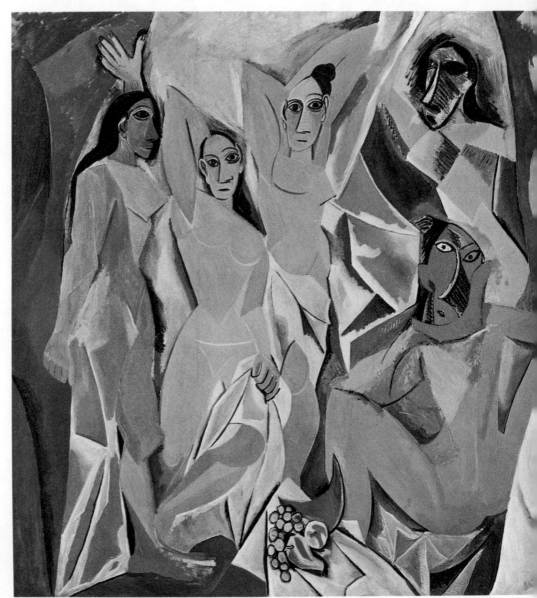

Pablo Picasso, *Les Demoiselles d'Avignon,* 1906–1907

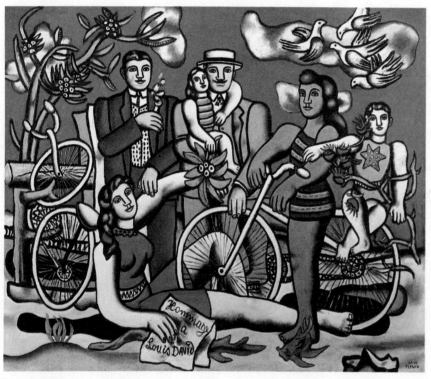

Fernand Léger, *Leisure*, 1944–49

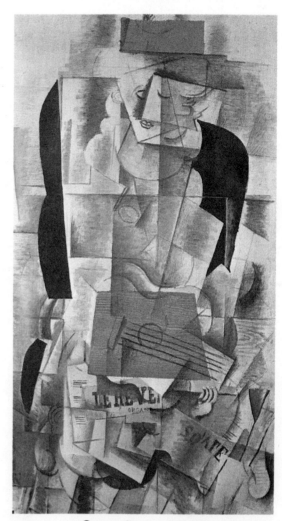

Georges Braque, *Girl with a Guitar*, 1911

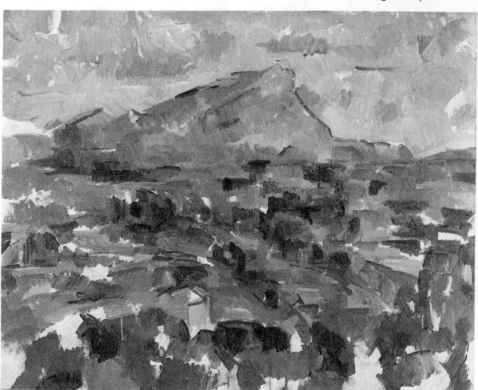

Paul Cézanne, *Mont Sainte Victoire*,
1904–1906

Henri Matisse was one of the most important artists of the first half of this century. His work has had a worldwide influence. He was a leader of the *Fauves*—a French word for "wild beasts." This referred to the group's use of bold, frequently distorted forms and wildly unrealistic colors. To some, their paintings appeared barbaric.

Marc Chagall is a Russian-born artist who worked in Paris. His typical paintings mix poetry and fantasy. In many of them he imaginatively relives the experiences of his childhood in Russia.

Chaim Soutine was born in Lithuania. He went to Paris to join the Expressionist group there. Success came to him slowly, but in 1913 the American collector Dr. Albert C. Barnes bought a hundred of his paintings. Soutine's life's work ranged from morbid and passionate interpretations of the world around him to, in his later years, the more decorative and glowing images he painted in the 1920s and 1930s.

Georges Rouault was an original member of the Fauves but he later turned from bright to more somber colors. He was an intensely devout Roman Catholic. As a boy he was apprenticed to a maker of stained glass. In later life he often looked to medieval art for subjects. This is evident in his portrait of Christ, *Behold the Man (Ecce Homo)*. Here the dark outlines that separate areas of color strongly recall the leaded joints of medieval windows.

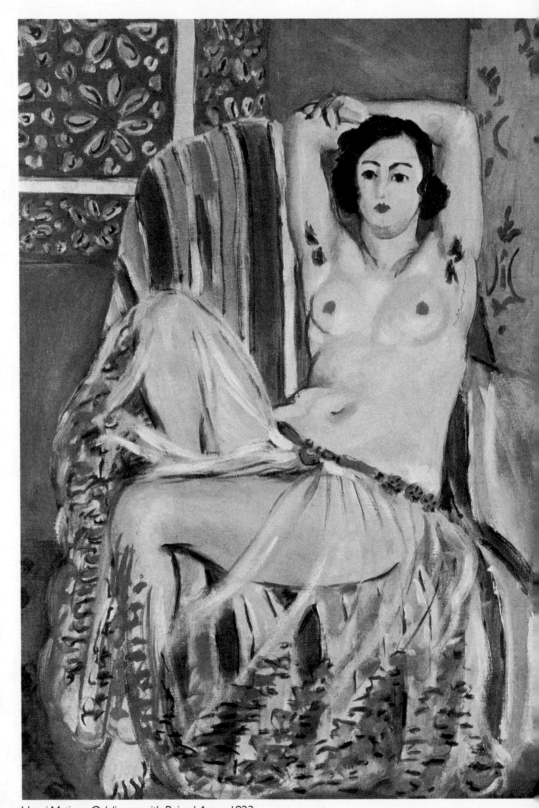

Henri Matisse, *Odalisque with Raised Arms*, 1923

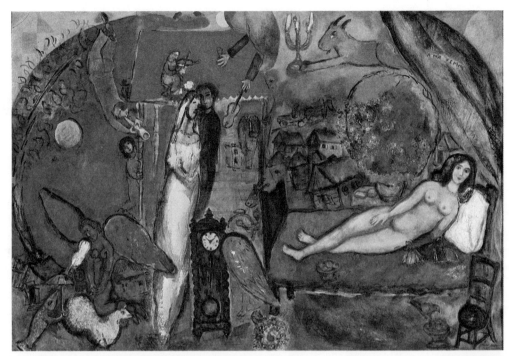

Marc Chagall, *To My Wife*, 1933–34

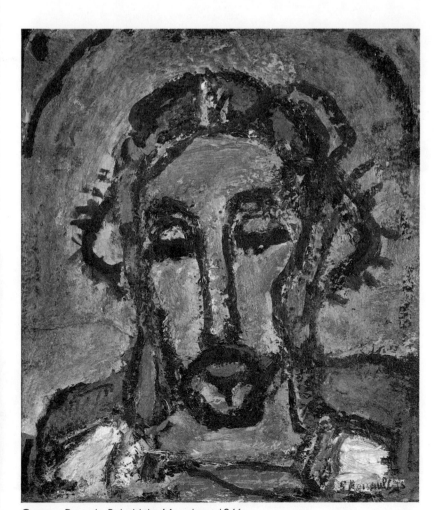

Georges Rouault, *Behold the Man*, about 1946

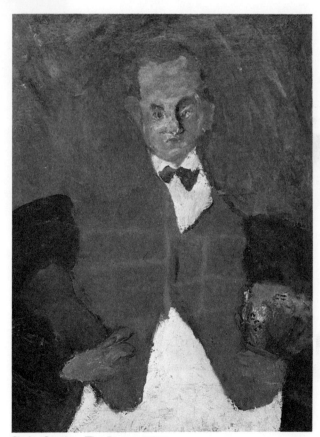

Chaim Soutine, *The Porter*, 1927

Like so many other foreign artists, the Italian **Amedeo Modigliani** was attracted to Paris. After an unhappy life, he died there at an early age. He was a gifted early 20th-century sculptor as well as a painter. In his work the gentle melancholy expressed with delicate lines distantly recalls the works of another Italian artist, Botticelli, five centuries earlier.

The paintings of the Swiss-born artist/musician **Paul Klee** are like signs intended to give some direction to a flight of our imagination, like brief sentences in paragraphs that have yet to be written out. In a very sophisticated way he tried to capture the spontaneity of children's drawings.

Alberto Giacometti was another Swiss-born artist. He was a sculptor and a painter. In his typical sculptures he produced dreamlike elongations of human forms, spirits in bronze.

Wassily Kandinsky was trained in Russia to be a lawyer. He turned to art and became a brilliant painter after he moved to Germany. There he became a leading member of a group called the Blue Horseman (der Blaue Reiter), who practiced Expressionism. He believed that art should be as abstract as music. In time he abandoned representation altogether. Using the free brushwork and bright colors of the Fauves, he developed a completely abstract style.

The Dutch artist **Piet Mondrian** studied in Paris before coming to America in 1934. He observed that all painting is composed of line and color and he characteristically reduced his works to just that in a very austere manner. He divided his canvas into rectangles of color separated by heavy black lines. It is purely abstract art executed with mathematical precision.

The American artist **Joseph Cornell** is best remembered for his small shadow-box constructions. In these shallow, glass-fronted containers he placed various kinds of found objects of no particular artistic interest but selected and arranged to evoke a pleasantly nostalgic mood, as in his *Soap Bubble Set.*

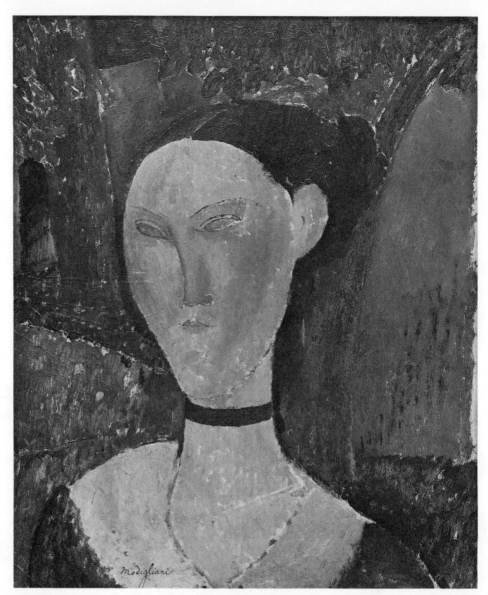

Amedeo Modigliani, *Woman with Velvet Ribbon*, 1915

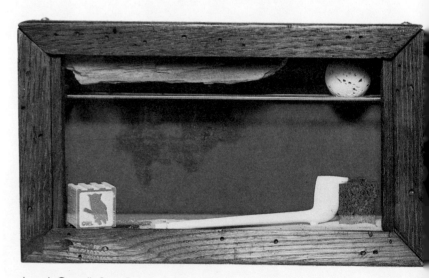

Joseph Cornell, *Soap Bubble Set*, box construction, about 1945

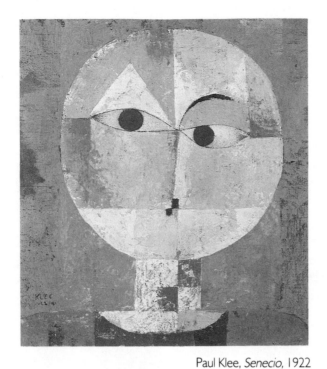

Paul Klee, *Senecio*, 1922

Alberto Giacometti,
Walking Man, 1947–48

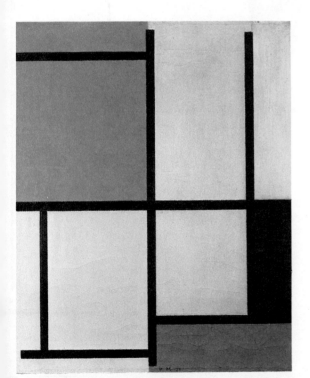

Piet Mondrian, *Composition*, 1921

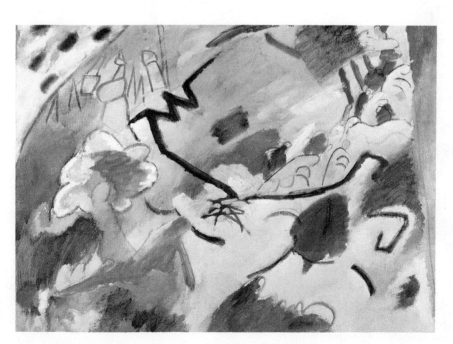

Wassily Kandinsky, *Improvisation with Horses*, 1911

Constantin Brancusi's beautifully tooled abstract brass sculpture *Bird in Space* has become a widely admired work of art. It first caught the attention of the American public when the United States Customs Service classified it as a taxable knickknack rather than as art. The government lost its case in a decision that received a lot of publicity. Brancusi's extreme simplification of form, his great craftsmanship, and the symbolic character of his subjects earned him a wide following.

Aristide Maillol was a well-known French sculptor and wood engraver. He is best remembered for his strong, energetic female nudes.

Having learned how to weld and assemble metal parts during World War II, the American sculptor **David Smith** forged the way for the development of constructed sculptures of iron and steel.

Henry Moore is the most notable British sculptor of our time. In many of his compositions, the hollowed-out areas are as important as the solid parts. He is known for his sculptures of family groups and reclining women. Moore is also a very skillful draftsman.

The characteristic works of the French artist **Jean Dubuffet** deliberately suggest such art as might be produced by children and visionaries.

The American sculptor **Louise Nevelson** was born in Russia. She has worked in many different styles. One popular phase of her art has been her placement of various found wooden objects within rectangular containers. In some of her sculptures these elements can be moved and rearranged in different compositions.

In *Horse and Rider,* Italian sculptor **Marino Marini** recalls scenes he observed in World War II of anxious peasants fleeing from air raids on their farm horses.

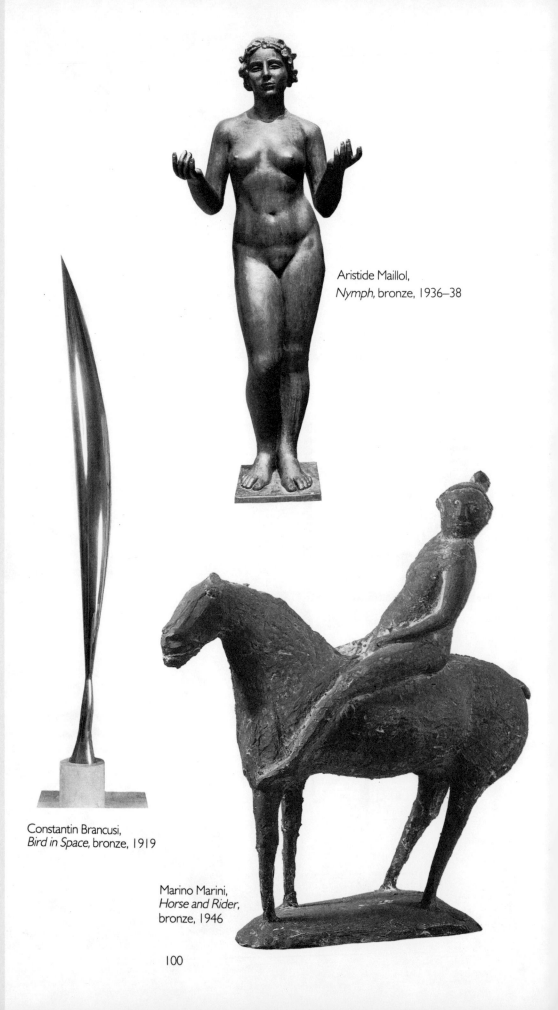

Aristide Maillol,
Nymph, bronze, 1936–38

Constantin Brancusi,
Bird in Space, bronze, 1919

Marino Marini,
Horse and Rider,
bronze, 1946

100

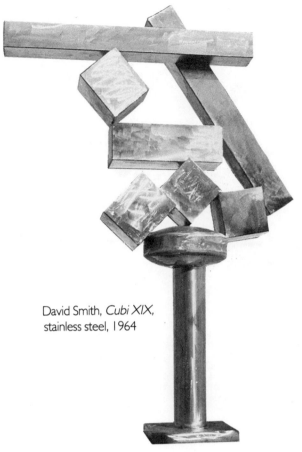

David Smith, *Cubi XIX*,
stainless steel, 1964

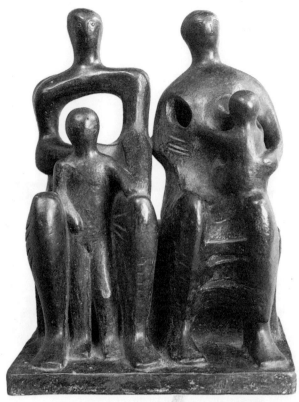

Henry Moore, *Family Group*, bronze, 1946

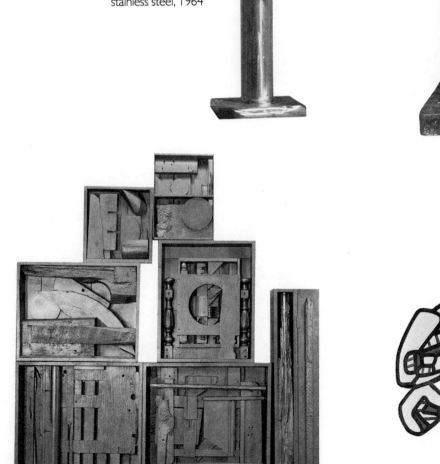

Louise Nevelson, *Unit of Seven*, wood, 1960

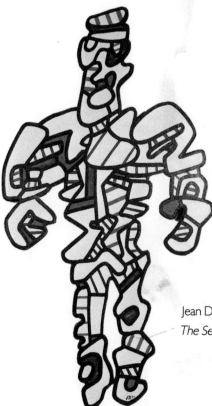

Jean Dubuffet,
The Sergeant, kiegecell, 1971

Edward Hopper was a modern American Realist. In almost all his significant works, light and the effect of light in all its variations provide the main dramatic element.

Ben Shahn came to America from Lithuania as a child. In the 1920s he produced a series of paintings based on the trial and execution of Sacco and Vanzetti, two anarchists whom the artist (and many others) thought were victims of injustice. The distortion and stylization of Shahn's portraits intensifies his characterization of the two doomed men.

Early in her career **Georgia O'Keeffe** discovered that she could say things with shapes and colors that she had no words for. She has long remained one of America's most original and forceful modern artists.

Andrew Wyeth has been producing acutely realistic paintings that continue to appeal to virtually everyone, from the general public to museum experts.

The style of the American artist **Jackson Pollock** is in total contrast to Wyeth's. After 1947 Pollock began to create his famous drip paintings. "The modern painter," he remarked, "cannot express his age, the airplane, the atom bomb, the radio, in the old forms of the Renaissance or any other culture." He laid a large canvas on the floor and walked around it, dribbling strands of color across the surface as he felt the urge. This is known as action painting.

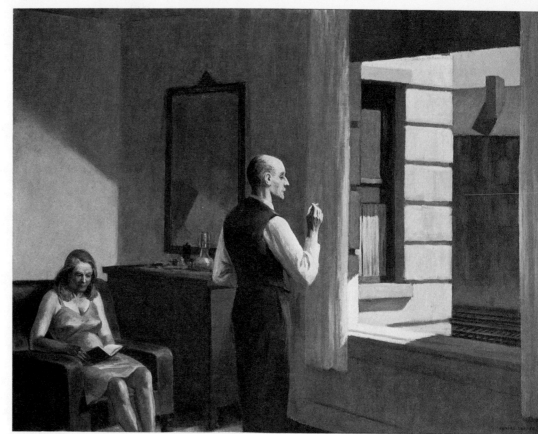

Edward Hopper, *Hotel by Railroad*, 1952

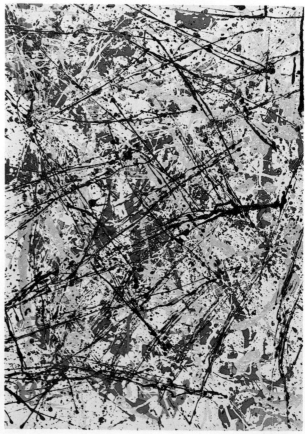

Jackson Pollock, untitled, 1949

102

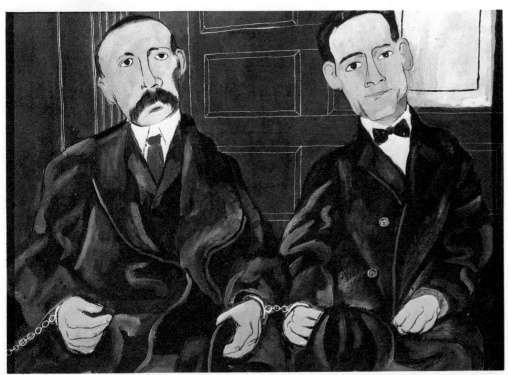

Ben Shahn, *Bartholomew Vanzetti and Nicholas Sacco*, 1931–32

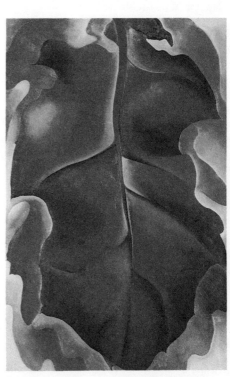

Georgia O'Keeffe,
Autumn Leaves #2, 1927

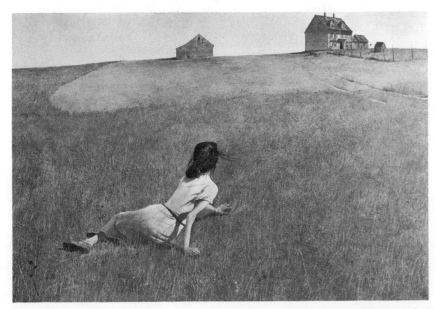

Andrew Wyeth, *Christina's World*, 1948

In the early 1960s a new style known as Pop Art burst on the American scene. As in **Robert Rauschenberg**'s *Sleep for Yvonne Rainer*, this art offered an alternative to abstract painting by including images of very commonplace things in loose and seemingly disorderly arrangements.

Morris Louis produced a great number of works in which he explored the basic problems of painting with pure colors.

German-born artist **Hans Hofmann** has had a great influence on modern American art through his teaching. One of his paintings, *Golden Splendor*—a turbulent outburst of color—reflects his belief that pictures should be made with feeling, not with knowing.

The works of the Russian-born American painter **Mark Rothko** typically feature large horizontal bars of thinned pigments. He was a leading interpreter of abstract expressionism.

While he was developing his personal style of painting, **Frank Stella** supported himself by working as a house painter. Like many other modern artists, he has experimented in numerous ways. To achieve special effects, he has sometimes painted canvases as large as ten feet high and twenty feet long.

To excite a viewer's imagination, **Jim Dine**, like Rauschenberg, sometimes attaches real three-dimensional objects to his canvases. He was a prominent exponent of Pop Art and shows a sense of humor in his work.

Robert Motherwell has practiced abstract painting since the beginning of his distinguished professional career. In doing so, he has approached this style of art from many directions. He has explained the principles of his art in a number of books and in his classroom teaching.

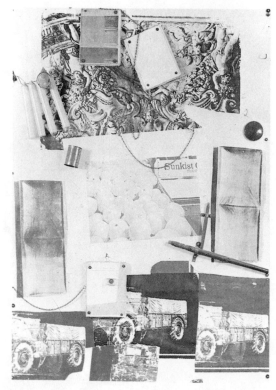

Robert Rauschenberg, *Sleep for Yvonne Rainer*, 1965

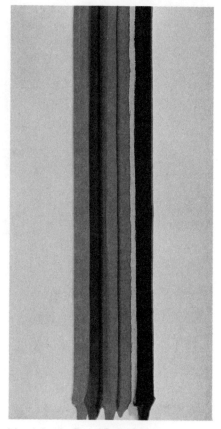

Morris Louis, *Flood End*, 1961

Robert Motherwell, *Open #29 in Crimson with Charcoal Line*, 1969

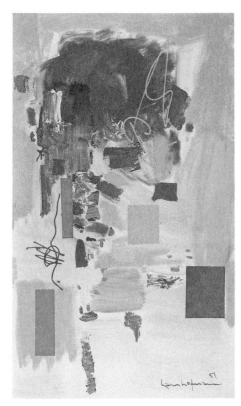

Hans Hofmann, *Golden Splendor*, 1957

Mark Rothko, untitled, 1960–61

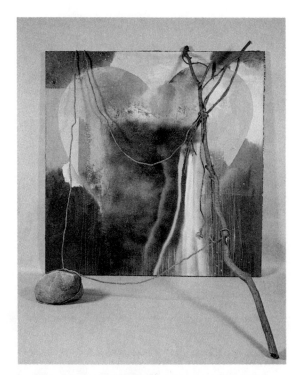

Jim Dine, *Heart with Rock, Branches, and Cord*, 1971

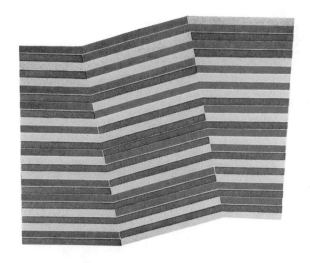

Frank Stella, *Bam*, 1966

INDEX OF ARTISTS

This biographical index lists some of the artists who have made significant contributions to the development of art. Where a page number is given, additional information can be found in the text.

ALBERS, JOSEF (1888–1976). A German-born artist who came to America to teach and to paint. He specialized in geometric compositions in the form of squares filled with subtly modulated colors.

ALBRIGHT, IVAN LE LORRAINE (1897–   ). An American painter whose painstakingly meticulous renderings of reality are filled with moral overtones.

ALLSTON, WASHINGTON (1779–1843). The first important American romantic landscape painter, and a central figure in the cultural life of New England. Teacher of the artist-inventor Samuel F. B. Morse.

ANGELICO, FRA (1387–1455). An artist of the Italian Renaissance. A devout monk, he painted a large number of religious subjects in the Dominican monasteries where he lived much of his life. In many of his best paintings he used clear, bright colors and gold.

ARCHIPENKO, ALEXANDER (1887–1964). A Ukrainian-American sculptor. He came to America in 1923 via Paris and Berlin. His nearly abstract figures earned him international recognition.

ARP, JEAN (1887–1966). A French painter and sculptor who created a wide variety of novel abstract works in the form of painted cutouts, collages, painted wood reliefs, and sculptures in the round. Some of these suggest organic forms and some are humorous.

AUDUBON, JOHN JAMES (1785–1851). See p. 78.

AVERY, MILTON (1893–1965). An American painter who characteristically reduced the human figure to flat patterns of color outlined by sharp rhythmic contours. His simplified, agreeably colored compositions recall the work of Matisse.

BASKIN, LEONARD (1922–   ). An American artist in different media. His woodcuts, often reproduced, are admired for their expressive power.

BECKMANN, MAX (1884–1950). An outstanding German painter and graphic artist who spent the last three years of his life teaching in New York.

BELLINI, GENTILE (1429–1507). Although not so well remembered as his brother, Giovanni (see below), this Bellini was an important Venetian artist of the Renaissance. In 1479 he was chosen to paint a portrait of the Sultan of Constantinople. While he was there he observed oriental architecture and costume, a knowledge reflected in his later work in Venice.

BELLINI, GIOVANNI (about 1430–1516). Considered by some to have been the greatest Venetian painter of the High Renaissance. He was the teacher of Titian and Giorgione and had great influence on the younger painters of his day. His older brother, Gentile, was also an important artist.

BENTON, THOMAS HART (1889–1975). A midwestern American artist whose work celebrates the wholesome quality of life in the heartland of this country.

BERNINI, GIOVANNI LORENZO (1598–1680). An outstanding Italian sculptor and architect of his time. His name will always be associated with his magnificent architectural contributions to St. Peter's Cathedral in Rome.

BINGHAM, GEORGE CALEB (1811–79). See p. 79.

BLAKE, WILLIAM (1757–1827). A visionary British painter and poet whose highly personal approach to art, both in his style and subject matter, had a power that was not fully appreciated until almost a century after his death.

BLAKELOCK, RALPH ALBERT (1847–1919). A largely self-taught American landscape artist whose typical paintings are poetic visions of a dark and mysterious world. He spent seventeen years in an insane asylum, during which time his work attracted increasing attention.

BOLDINI, GIOVANNI (1842–1931). An Italian portraitist who, at the peak of his fame, was commissioned to paint romanticized likenesses of celebrities.

BONHEUR, ROSA (1822–99). A French painter of animals, in which specialty she was very successful. Her best-known work is her gigantic *Horse Fair*.

BONNARD, PIERRE (1867–1947). A French artist whose decorative interior views are imaginative blends of form and color.

BOSCH, HIERONYMUS (working 1488–1516). See p. 57.

BOTTICELLI, SANDRO (about 1444–1510). See p. 45.

BOUCHER, FRANÇOIS (1703–70). The most popular French artist of the mid-18th century. Boucher became the president of the Royal Academy, first painter to King Louis XV, and favorite and tutor of the influential Madame de Pompadour. His paintings of seductive nudes, who were sometimes posed as goddesses, were well suited to the taste of the courtly circles of the time.

BOUGUEREAU, ADOLPHE WILLIAM (1825–1905). A fashionable French artist whose almost photographically accurate paintings showed no regard for the art of his day. His glossy nudes were much admired.

BOUTS, DIRK (about 1415–75). A Flemish painter whose art recalls the work of Van Eyck and Van der Weyden.

BRANCUSI, CONSTANTIN (1876–1957). See p. 100.

BRAQUE, GEORGES (1882–1963). See p. 95.

BREUGHEL, JAN (1568–1625). Son of Pieter Bruegel. Called "Velvet" because of the remarkably polished finish of his paintings. Admired by Rubens, with whom he sometimes collaborated.

BRONZINO, AGNOLO (1503–72). See p. 52.

BROUWER, ADRIAEN (1605/6–38). A prominent Flemish painter who represented common everyday life. In his later work especially, peasants are shown as very ordinary, coarse folk. He had many followers.

BRUEGEL THE ELDER, PIETER (1525/30–69). See p. 58.

BURCHFIELD, CHARLES (1893–1967). An American painter who usually worked in watercolor. Is well known for his lyric scenes of nature as well as for his haunting views of late-19th-century small-town America, as such communities were fading with time.

BURNE-JONES, EDWARD COLEY (1839–98). A British painter and decorator associated with the influential reformer William Morris and the Pre-Raphaelite group.

CALDER, ALEXANDER (1898–1976). An inventive American sculptor very well known for his mobiles (made of parts that move) and stabiles (abstract compositions with no movable parts).

CAMPIN, ROBERT (about 1375/78–1444). Sometimes identified as the Master of Flémalle. See p. 55.

CANALETTO (GIOVANNI ANTONIO CANAL, 1697–1768). See p. 72.

CARAVAGGIO, MICHELANGELO MERISI DA (1570/73–1610). See p. 53.

CARPACCIO, VITTORE (about 1455–1526). A Venetian artist whose paintings emphasize minute details and glowing, enamel-like surfaces. His depictions of sacred and other legends use contemporary Venice for a background and are peopled by Venetians in rich, bright costumes.

CARRACCI, AGOSTINO (1557–1602). A painter from Bologna, Italy, cousin of Ludovico Carracci (1555–1619) and brother of Annibale Carracci (1560–1609). The three founded an important academy of art and sometimes worked together. Agostino was a talented engraver as well as a painter. He ended his days in a monastery.

CASSATT, MARY (1854–1926). See p. 88.

CASTAGNO, ANDREA DEL (about 1423–57). An Italian artist with a so

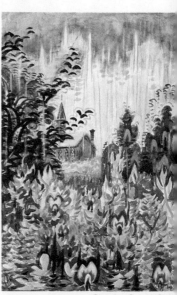

Charles Burchfield

ific interest in perspective, which
used to create deceptive illusions
space.

TLIN, GEORGE (1796–1872). A
-taught American painter best
own for his studies of Indian life.

LLINI, BENVENUTO (1500–71).
p. 49.

ZANNE, PAUL (1839–1906). See
5.

AGALL, MARC (1887–   ).
p. 97.

**HARDIN, JEAN-BAPTISTE-
ÉON** (1699–1779). See p. 68.

IRICO, GIORGIO DE. See de
rico, Giorgio.

RISTUS, PETRUS (about 1415–
73). A Flemish painter whose
rks recall those of Van Eyck and
der Weyden.

MABUE (CENNI DI PEPO, about
0–about 1302). See p. 29.

AUDE LORRAINE. See Lorraine,
ude.

OUET, FRANÇOIS (before
2–72). A French court painter.
ous in his day for his many excel-
portraits of kings, nobles, and
er personages. His father, Fran-
, was also an artist.

OLE, THOMAS (1801–48). An
lish-born artist who, after coming
America as a teenager, became a
ding painter of the Hudson River
ool. His work ranged from metic-
usly rendered landscapes to large,
lly painted subjects with moralistic
ssages.

NSTABLE, JOHN (1776–1837).
p. 77.

PLEY, JOHN SINGLETON
38–1815). See p. 74.

RNELL, JOSEPH (1903–72). See
8.

**ROT, CAMILLE JEAN BAP-
TE** (1796–1875). An important
nch painter, principally of land-
pes. His work was transitional be-
een the classical compositions of
early 19th century and later ro-
ntic interpretations of nature.

**RREGGIO (ANTONIO ALLE-
I DA,** 1489/94–1534). Italian
ter of the High Renaissance whose
rk served as an introduction to the
oque style.

URBET, GUSTAVE (1819–77).
p. 81.

COVARRUBIAS, MIGUEL (1904?–
57). A Mexican-born American
painter. Well known as an illustrator,
stage designer, and caricaturist.

CRANACH THE ELDER, LUCAS
(1472–1553). A German-born artist
who with the help of his son and other
associates produced a large number
of portraits of notable contemporaries. Worked largely in Vienna. A close
friend of Martin Luther's.

CRIVELLI, CARLO (about 1430–95).
An Italian painter principally of religious subjects. His work is often richly
ornamented with realistic and colorful garlands of fruit and vegetables.

CROPSEY, JASPER FRANCIS (1823–
1900). An American landscapist of the
Hudson River School, well regarded
for his autumnal views of the Catskills
and the White Mountains.

CURRY, JOHN STEUART (1897–
1946). Associated with Grant Wood
and Thomas Hart Benton as one of
the leading painters of a regional
movement of the 1930s that focused
on midwestern subjects.

DADDI, BERNARDO (active about
1320–50). One of the most important Florentine followers of Giotto.

DALI, SALVADOR (1904–   ).
A Spanish painter and illustrator,
whose subjects suggest strange
dreams. Forms are distorted and
shown in unnatural combinations.

**DAUBIGNY, CHARLES FRAN-
ÇOIS** (1817–78). An early out-of-
doors French painter who floated in

a special boat while composing his
river scenes. Had a direct influence
on the Impressionists.

DAUMIER, HONORÉ (1808–79).
See p. 81.

DAVID, GERARD (about 1460–
1523). A Flemish artist, largely of religious subjects, who worked mostly in
Bruges. Influenced by Jan van Eyck.
Combined naturalism and idealiza-
tion in his luminous paintings.

DAVID, JACQUES-LOUIS (1748–
1825). See p. 72.

DAVIES, ARTHUR BOWEN (1862–
1928). An American artist whose
most typical works are romantic in
mood, featuring ghostly figures in lyrical, dreamlike situations.

DA VINCI, LEONARDO (1452–
1519). See pp. 49, 50.

DE CHIRICO, GIORGIO (1888–
1978). A Greek-born Italian artist who
also worked in Germany and France.
The dreamlike, supernatural character of his work evokes an atmosphere of mystery and loneliness.
Probably the most influential Italian
artist of the 20th century.

**DEGAS (HILAIRE EDGAR DE
GAS,** 1834–1917). See p. 87.

DE HOOCH, PIETER (1629–after
1688). A Dutch artist best known for
his paintings of middle-class daily life.

DE KOONING, WILLEM (1904–
). A prominent Dutch-born
abstract painter who came to America as a young man.

DELACROIX, FERDINAND VIC-

TOR EUGÈNE (1798–1863). A
leading French artist of the Romantic
movement and an intimate friend of
Géricault's. He painted a wide variety
of subjects, many of them charged
with emotional force.

DELAUNAY, ROBERT (1885–1941).
A French painter who was involved
in various phases of modern art both
before and after World War I. His
imaginative use of pure, vibrant colors
in his work influenced a number of
his distinguished contemporaries, both
European and American.

DELLA FRANCESCA, PIERO. See
Piero della Francesca.

DEL SARTO, ANDREA (1486–
1531). A greatly skilled Italian painter
of the High Renaissance whose works
show the influence of Leonardo da
Vinci and Michelangelo, but little of
the vital inspiration that guided those
great contemporaries. He was a brilliant colorist whose own influence can
be seen in Italian art of the following
generation.

DEMUTH, CHARLES (1883–1935).
A pioneer in modern American art
who worked variously in watercolor,
tempera, and oil. His paintings, rang-
ing in subject from delicate floral forms
to industrial architecture, are pre-
cisely rendered.

DERAIN, ANDRÉ (1880–1954). A
French modernist who before World
War I was one of the original group
of Fauves (a word meaning "wild
beasts"), which included Matisse and
Vlaminck, among others, and which
used intense color and distorted forms
for emotional and decorative effects.

DI COSIMO, PIERO. See Piero di
Cosimo.

DINE, JIM (1935–   ). See p. 105.

DOMENICO, VENEZIANO (working about 1438–61). A Florentine
painter in whose work color, perspective, landscape, and light were incorporated in a distinctively lyrical
manner.

**DONATELLO (DONATO DI NIC-
COLÒ,** 1386–1466). See p. 44.

**DOSSO, DOSSI (GIOVANNI LU-
TERI,** about 1480–1542). An Italian
painter best remembered for his romantic landscapes, which are unusual
in Italian art of the time.

DOU, GERARD (1613–75). An early
student of Rembrandt's, who painted
portraits and peasant scenes with a

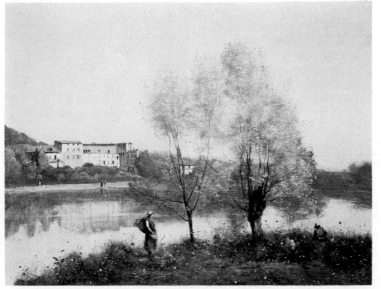

Camille Corot

convincing accuracy that made him one of the highest-paid artists of his day.

DOUGHTY, THOMAS (1783–1856). One of the earliest American landscapists. For the most part he was self-taught. A prominent member of the Hudson River School.

DOVE, ARTHUR GARFIELD (1880–1946). An American artist who, after several years of study in Europe, returned to the United States to paint the first American abstract picture.

DUBUFFET, JEAN (1901–   ). See p. 101.

DUCCIO DI BUONINSEGNA (about 1255–1319). A great master of early Italian art. In June 1311, when his altarpiece portraying the Madonna was triumphantly carried through the streets of Siena from his workshop to the cathedral, it was cause for a citywide celebration. He had many followers.

DUCHAMP, MARCEL (1887–1968). See p. 92.

DUFY, RAOUL (1877–1953). A French painter whose colorful works, full of life and movement, became very fashionable. Also designed fabrics, tapestries, and ceramics.

DURAND, ASHER BROWN (1796–1886). See p. 78.

DÜRER, ALBRECHT (1471–1528). See p. 56.

EAKINS, THOMAS (1844–1916). See p. 89.

EARL, RALPH (1751–1801). A self-taught itinerant American portraitist and landscape artist.

ENSOR, JAMES (1860–1949). A productive and original modern Belgian painter and etcher; one of the great innovators of the late 19th century. His work was once considered gruesome and scandalous, but it opened the way for modern dream-like paintings.

ERNST, MAX (1891–1976). A leading German painter who used pasted-on fragments and rubbings of objects to evoke new associations of shapes, ideas, and textures.

FANTIN-LATOUR, HENRI (1836–1904). See p. 80.

FEININGER, LYONEL (1871–1956). An American-born artist who lived in France and Germany for many years

but who fled Europe with the coming of Hitler. He developed a delicate geometric style often featuring sailboats and skyscrapers.

FOUQUET, JEAN (1420–77/81). A French painter to the court. His important early work included a portrait of King Charles VII, whose victorious armies were led by Joan of Arc against the British invaders of France.

FRAGONARD, JEAN-HONORÉ (1732–1806). See p. 71.

FUSELI, (JOHN) HENRY (1741–1825). A Swiss-born painter who spent most of his life in London. The weird and grotesque character of his imaginative design was strongly influenced by William Blake.

GAINSBOROUGH, THOMAS (1727–88). See p. 71.

GAUGUIN, PAUL (1848–1903). See p. 91.

GENTILE DA FABRIANO (about 1370–1427). An Italian artist who worked in a number of different cities and whose influence was felt throughout that land. His paintings carry over late medieval traditions in a style that was followed in many parts of Europe.

GÉRICAULT, JEAN LOUIS ANDRÉ THÉODORE (1791–1824). See p. 76.

GHIRLANDAIO, DOMENICO (1452–94). See p. 44.

GIACOMETTI, ALBERTO (1901–66). See p. 99.

GIORGIONE DA CASTELFRANCO (1478–1510). See p. 53.

GIOTTO DI BONDONE (about 1266–1337). See p. 40.

GLACKENS, WILLIAM JAMES (1870–1938). An original member of the so-called Ashcan School, or The Eight. Like others of that group, he worked for a number of years as a newspaper and magazine illustrator.

GOES, HUGO VAN DER. See van der Goes, Hugo.

GOTTLIEB, ADOLPH (1903–74). An American abstract painter who used geometric and symbolic shapes to make his personal statements.

GOYA, FRANCISCO DE (1746–1820). See p. 73.

GOZZOLI, BENOZZO (1420–92). See p. 42.

GRAVES, MORRIS (1910–   ). An American artist whose work has

been influenced by his studies of Zen Buddhism and oriental art. There is mystery and magic in his depictions of strange, unreal "spirit birds," as he has called them.

EL GRECO (DOMENICO THEOTOCOPOULOUS, 1541–1614). See p. 65.

GREUZE, JEAN BAPTISTE (1725–1805). A French artist whose sentimental paintings characteristically praised the virtues of simple domestic life, when other French painters were depicting the gay frivolities of the aristocracy. He was also a fine portraitist and painted a likeness of Benjamin Franklin.

GRIS, JUAN (1887–1927). A Spanish-born artist who worked the last twenty-one years of his life in Paris and painted in a highly original manner. Created stage sets for the Ballet Russe.

GROSZ, GEORGE (1893–1959). One of a number of German artists who fled to America to escape Nazism. In his native land he savagely satirized the government and its army, often with a bitter humor that added a cutting edge to the horrors he depicted.

GRÜNEWALD, MATTHIAS (1475/80–1528). One of the greatest Northern European painters of his day. His masterpiece, the Isenheim

Altarpiece, is considered by many to be the finest work of German art.

GUARDI, FRANCESCO (1712–9?). A Venetian painter who was wide patronized by aristocratic Englis men. His views of his native city ar the pageantry of life there were mu admired and formed his stock in trad

GUYS, CONSTANTIN (1802/5–9). A French painter well known for wash drawings of Parisian women dubious virtue. His works are wi and charming.

GWATHMEY, ROBERT (190?). A modern Americ painter principally of southern bla life, which he depicts with a deep ser of social justice.

HALS, FRANS (1580/81–1666). S p. 62.

HARDING, CHESTER (1792–186? A self-taught American portrait Painted likenesses of a number notable Americans.

HARNETT, WILLIAM MICHA (1848–92). See p. 81.

HARTLEY, MARSDEN (1877–194 A pioneer of modern art in Americ His paintings are rich with stylized na ural forms, boldly structured and c ored.

HASSAM, CHILDE (1859–1935). American Impressionist whose pai ings sparkle with vibrant colors.

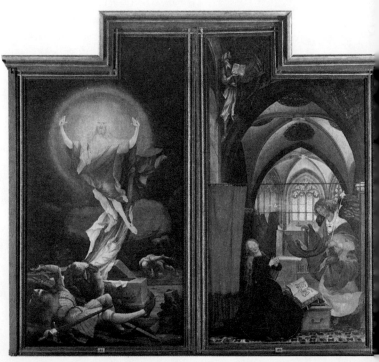

Matthias Grünewa

HEADE, MARTIN JOHNSON (1819–1904). An American artist of luminously colored marine subjects. Heade also painted pictures of the exotic fauna and flora of Brazil's rain forests.

HENRI, ROBERT (1865–1929). A member of the Ashcan School. An influential and prominent portraitist.

HICKS, EDWARD (1780–1849). A self-taught American painter best remembered for his many naive and charming renderings of *The Peaceable Kingdom*.

HOFMANN, HANS (1880–1966). See p. 105.

HOGARTH, WILLIAM (1697–1764). See p. 70.

HOLBEIN THE YOUNGER, HANS (1497/98–1543). See p. 61.

HOMER, WINSLOW (1836–1910). See p. 89.

HOOCH, PIETER DE. See de Hooch, Pieter.

HOPPER, EDWARD (1882–1967). See p. 103.

HOUDON, JEAN-ANTOINE (1741–1828). See p. 71.

HOVENDEN, THOMAS (1840–95). An Irish-born American painter of scenes from sentimental stories that were in vogue at the time. His *Breaking Home Ties* was immensely popular.

INGRES, JEAN AUGUST DOMINIQUE (1780–1867). A French painter who turned to classical art for inspiration. He spent a number of years in Italy and later became a teacher. An outstanding feature of his style is his reliance on linear patterns which are admired for their own sake regardless of the subject.

INNESS, GEORGE (1825–94). An American artist best remembered for his landscapes. In his later work these became poetic, almost mystical visions of the beauty of nature.

JOHNS, JASPER (1910–). An American artist whose work heralded the Pop Art movement. Johns has used commonplace things like flags and beer cans as his subjects, presenting them for our consideration as objects of art. He sometimes also attaches real objects such as brooms and rulers to his canvases to vary his images.

JOHNSON, EASTMAN (1824–1906). A versatile American painter who studied in Germany and, before returning to his native land, worked in The Hague, where he made a distinguished reputation. His later spirited scenes of the American countryside were and still are widely admired.

KANDINSKY, WASSILY (1866–1944). See p. 99.

KENSETT, JOHN FREDERICK (1818–72). A popular American landscapist in the tradition of the Hudson River School. His use of luminous colors brought him close to Impressionism, although he never broke up his colors into flecks of light, as the Impressionists did.

KENT, ROCKWELL (1882–1971). A popular American painter and illustrator whose vigorous renderings of nature's grandeur drew on his travels from the Arctic to the Antarctic.

KLEE, PAUL (1879–1940). See p. 99.

KOKOSCHKA, OSKAR (1886–1980). A very versatile Austrian artist, writer, and teacher. His paintings were banned by the Nazis, from whose regime he was forced to flee. His work made use of distortions of form, color, and space to express the inner truth of his subjects.

KOLLWITZ, KÄTHE (1867–1945). A German artist whose sculptures and graphics made her an important figure in the arts of her time.

KOONING, WILLEM DE. See De Kooning, Willem.

LACHAISE, GASTON (1882–1935). A French sculptor who left Paris for New York in 1906. Made a unique contribution to modern sculpture with his large, robust, and voluptuous nudes with which he celebrated his vision of woman. One is reminded of the *Venus of Willendorf* (see p. 6).

LA FARGE, JOHN (1835–1910). An American painter and designer of stained glass. Studied abroad in various countries. His later work was influenced by the scenes he saw during a visit to the Orient and the South Seas. He also influenced American culture through his writings, lectures, and teaching.

LANE, FITZ HUGH (1804–65). America's first native-born marine painter of merit, Lane was a skilled draftsman who was sensitive to the changing moods of sea and sky and recorded them in subtle colors.

LATOUR, GEORGES DE (1593–1652). A French painter of largely religious subjects which are often dramatically lighted by a shielded candle. For years after his death his work was attributed to Le Nain, Vermeer, and others.

LAURENCIN, MARIE (1885–1956). French painter and graphic artist. Her work is pleasantly decorative.

LÉGER, FERNAND (1881–1955). See p. 95.

LE NAIN, LOUIS (about 1593–1648). See p. 65.

LEONARDO DA VINCI. See da Vinci, Leonardo.

LEUTZE, EMANUEL (1816–68). A German-born artist who worked in America. Remembered principally for his huge canvas *Washington Crossing the Delaware*.

LIMBOURG BROTHERS. See p. 36.

LIPPI, FRA FILIPPO (about 1406–69). A Florentine early Renaissance artist whose lyrical and lovely paintings of the Madonna and Child bring to mind similar works by Fra Angelico. Many great Italian masters, including Botticelli, Ghirlandaio, and da Vinci, were influenced by his work. A friend of the Medici family's.

LONGHI, PIETRO (1702–85). A Venetian artist whose paintings offer charming views of contemporary everyday life. Other painters of similar subjects followed his lead.

LORENZETTI, AMBROGIO (active 1305–48). See p. 40.

LORRAINE, CLAUDE (1600–82). A French landscapist whose romantic views of the countryside are painted with an intimate understanding of nature. His deft, colorful renderings of outdoor scenes and the surrounding atmosphere in some ways anticipate the Impressionists two centuries later.

LOUIS, MORRIS (1912–62). See p. 104.

LUKS, GEORGE BENJAMIN (1867–1933). A founder of the Ashcan School who, like others of this group, worked as a newspaper and magazine illustrator. His realistic paintings include dramatic, vigorously rendered views of New York's Lower East Side.

MAGNASCO, ALESSANDRO (1667–1749). An Italian painter with a very individual and complex style: dashing, explosive brushwork and a mixture of small, drawn-out figures and eerie, wind-torn landscapes shown in flickering light.

MAGRITTE, RENÉ (1898–1967). A Belgian painter whose works remind one of dreams.

MAILLOL, ARISTIDE (1861–1944). See p. 100.

MANET, EDOUARD (1832–83). See p. 83.

MANTEGNA, ANDREA (1431–1506). An important North Italian artist whose paintings show a remarkable understanding of perspective. He was a dedicated student of antiquity; his knowledge of classical architecture and costume was used to advantage in his painting.

MARC, FRANZ (1880–1916). A student of philology and theology who turned to painting in 1900 and created numerous images of horses, fawns, and other animals as symbols of a higher type of humanity.

MARIN, JOHN (1870–1953). See p. 93.

MARINI, MARINO (1901–80). See p. 100.

MARSH, REGINALD (1898–1954). An American painter who found his favorite subjects in the teeming activity of daily life in New York City. His crowded scenes of people at work or play are complex compositions, alive with action.

MARTIN, HOMER DODGE (1836–97). American landscapist who worked in France, where he was influenced by the paintings of Corot. He continued to paint while he was almost blind.

MARTINI, SIMONE (about 1284–1344). See p. 41.

MASACCIO (TOMMASO GUIDI, 1401–about 1428). See p. 46.

MATISSE, HENRI (1869–1954). See p. 96.

MEMLING, HANS (about 1435–94). A German-born Flemish painter. His intensely realistic portraits are among the masterpieces of Flemish art. The same attention to minute realistic detail characterizes his celebrated religious paintings.

METSYS, QUENTIN (1466–1530). See p. 56.

MICHELANGELO BUONAROTTI (1475–1564). See pp. 46, 47, 48.

MILLET, JEAN-FRANÇOIS (1814–75). See p. 80.

MIRÓ, JOAN (1893–). Born in Spain and moved to Paris as a young man. His very colorful works are further brightened by humorous imagination and unlikely exaggerations.

MODIGLIANI, AMADEO (1884–1920). See p. 98.

MONDRIAN, PIET (1872–1944). See p. 99.

MONET, CLAUDE (1840–1926). See p. 86.

MOORE, HENRY (1898–). See p. 101.

MORAN, THOMAS (1837–1926). An English-born American landscapist. His dramatically painted views of the American West were very popular.

MORISOT, BERTHE (1841–1895). A French woman member of the Impressionist movement.

MORRIS, WILLIAM (1834–1896). A British painter and poet and founder of the Arts and Crafts movement. It was a revival of creating household objects by hand in opposition to the machine-made productions of Morris's day.

MORSE, SAMUEL F. B. (1791–1872). See p. 75.

MOSES, ANNA MARY "GRAND-MA" ROBERTSON (1860–1961). An untutored American artist who took up painting at the age of 76 and soon became widely known and well liked.

MOTHERWELL, ROBERT (1915–). See p. 104.

MOUNT, WILLIAM SIDNEY (1807–68). One of the earliest American painters to depict the daily life of his countrymen, mostly as he witnessed it on rural Long Island. Some of his works were reproduced and widely distributed by the popular printmakers Currier & Ives.

MUNCH, EDVARD (1863–1944). See p. 91.

MURILLO, BARTOLOMÉ ESTEBAN (1616–82). A popular Spanish artist of the Baroque period. Demand for his religious works obliged him to operate a busy workshop. He died at the age of 66 as a result of a fall from a scaffold while he was painting a large mural for a convent in Cadiz.

NATTIER, JEAN-MARC (1685–1766). Leading court portraitist of King Louis XV of France. Also painted for the Russian royal family. He was particularly successful with his portraits of beautiful young women, often painting them in the roles of mythological figures.

NEGROLI, GIOVANNI PAOLO (active in the 16th century). See p. 49.

NEVELSON, LOUISE (1899–). See p. 101.

NOGUCHI, ISAMU (1904–). An American abstract sculptor of Japanese descent, who also created stage designs for the Martha Graham dance company.

NOLDE, EMIL (EMIL HANSEN, 1867–1956). A prominent German painter.

O'KEEFFE, GEORGIA (1887–). See p. 103.

ORCAGNA (ANDREA DI CIONE, about 1308–after 1368). Possibly the greatest Florentine painter of the second half of the 14th century. Few of his works have survived in good condition. He was also a sculptor and an architect.

OROZCO, JOSÉ CLEMENTE (1883–1949). A noted Mexican muralist who also produced memorable easel paintings, drawings, and lithographs. His compassionate views of the Mexican scene and its people won him distinction and popular favor.

PALMA VECCHIO (JACOMO NEGRETI, about 1480–1528). A Venetian artist who studied under Giovanni Bellini. He shared a love of color with other Venetian artists of his day.

PARMIGIANINO (GIROLAMO FRANCESCO MARIA MAZZOLA, 1503–40). A leading Italian Mannerist with elegantly dressed and posed subjects. Engravings of his drawings influenced the work of other artists in Florence and Venice, and later at Fontainebleau in France.

PATINIR, JOACHIM DE (about 1485–1524). A Flemish landscapist whose paintings anticipated those of Bruegel. He collaborated with several artists, who executed the figures for his backgrounds. He was a good friend of Dürer's.

PEALE, CHARLES WILLSON (1741–1827). See p. 75.

PERUGINO, PIETRO (about 1450–1523). During the last several decades of the 15th century Perugino was one of Italy's most esteemed painters. His importance is heightened by the fact that he was Raphael's teacher and had a major influence on that artist's school.

PICASSO, PABLO (1881–1973). See pp. 7, 94.

PIERO DELLA FRANCESCA (about 1416–92). One of the major artists of the Italian Renaissance. His frescoes known as *The Legend of the True Cross* are considered his major work. Later in life he ceased painting and wrote treatises on perspective and mathematics in which he contended that the invisible world could be reduced to mathematical order in art.

PIERO DI COSIMO (1462–1521). An inventive painter of the Italian Renaissance whose style is highly original. His association with the literary group around Lorenzo de Medici is reflected in some of his allegorical panels. He worked on the frescoes in the Sistine Chapel in the Vatican.

PINTURICCHIO (BERNARDINO DI BETTO, 1454–1513). A little man, as is implied by his nickname, by which he is best remembered. Pinturicchio was primarily a decorative muralist. He enjoyed the patronage of three different popes and contributed to the frescoes in the Sistine Chapel.

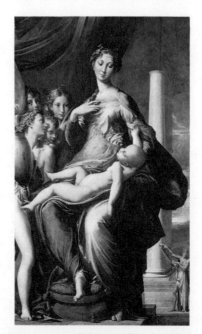

Francesco Parmigianino

PIRANESI, GIOVANNI BATTIST (1720–88). Important principally his melodramatic engravings based ancient Roman architectural scer and ruins. In these reconstructio Piranesi used contrasting light and d areas with vivid and free imaginatio

PISANELLO (ANTONIO PISAN about 1397–1455). A reputable I ian painter whose most import contributions were his portrait me als of many renowned people of time, such as the Byzantine empe and the king of Naples.

PISSARRO, CAMILLE (1831–190 Prominently involved with the star the French Impressionist moveme Friend of Monet's, Cézanne's, and Gogh's.

POLLAIUOLO, ANTONIO (143 98). An artist of many different tale whose paintings and engravings full of force and movement and play his keen interest in the hun body in action. His style is summ rized in his celebrated engraving *Battle of Nude Men*.

POLLOCK, JACKSON (1912– See pp. 2, 102.

PONTORMO, JACOPO DA (COPO CARUCCI, 1494–1557 neurotic and original genius who ceived a number of commissions fr the Medici family. In his later ye he was strongly influenced Michelangelo.

POUSSIN, NICOLAS (1594–16 See p. 65.

PRATT, MATTHEW (1734–18 An American artist best reme bered for his painting *The Amer School,* showing Benjamin West several of the many students came to study in West's Lon studio.

PRAXITELES (4th century B.C.). most celebrated of the ancient Gr sculptors. His most renowned wo are either entirely lost or rem bered only in Roman imitations. reputation seems forever fi through the praise heaped upor statues by his contemporaries.

PRENDERGAST, MAURICE B ZIL (1859–1924). See p. 93.

PRIMATICCIO, FRANCES (1504–70). An Italian artist celebra for his work at the French royal ace at Fontainebleau, both of w were commissioned by Francis his paintings he used exagger proportion and movement to produce an elegant, decorative style.

[PU]VIS DE CHAVANNES, PIERRE [CÉ]CILE (1824–98). A French painter [re]membered for his numerous mu[rals], in which the subjects are defined [by] quiet, linear patterns. His allegorical [pai]ntings to accompany the great [stai]rcase of the Boston Public Library [are] fine examples of his work.

[RA]EBURN, HENRY (1756–1823). A [Sc]ottish portraitist who painted his [sub]jects in a simple, straightforward [ma]nner.

[RA]PHAEL (1488–1520). See p. 51.

[RA]USCHENBERG, ROBERT [(19]25–). See p. 104.

[RE]DON, ODILON (1840–1916). A [Fre]nch painter for whom art meant [clo]thing the idea with form." With his [br]ush he explored his dream world.

[RE]MBRANDT HARMENSZOON [VA]N RIJN (1606–69). See p. 63.

[RE]MINGTON, FREDERIC (1861–[19]09). The best-known American [pai]nter and sculptor of the Far West. [His] work is intensely and dramatically [rea]listic. From it we have formed our [us]ual images of the last frontier with [its] cowboys, Indians, and cavalry.

[REN]I, GUIDO (1575–1642). An Italian [b]aroque painter whose work, al[tho]ugh now out of favor, was greatly [adm]ired by his contemporaries.

[RE]NOIR, PIERRE AUGUSTE (1841–[19]9). See p. 87.

[RE]YNOLDS, JOSHUA (1723–92). A [pro]lific British portraitist and historical [pai]nter. In 1764 he was named first [pre]sident of the Royal Academy and [in 1]784 principal painter to the king. [For] two decades he remained the [mo]st prominent if not the best artist [in t]he British Isles.

[RI]BALTA, FRANCISCO (1555–[9]8). An important Spanish painter [w]hose work the influence of Car[ava]ggio is clearly evident. Ribalta's own [dist]inctive style affected the develop[me]nt of Spanish naturalism.

[RIB]ERA, JUSEPE DE (about 1590–[16]52). A Spanish-born artist who set[tled] in Naples. He was esteemed as a [mo]st distinguished follower of Cara[va]gio. A good number of his paint[ing]s were commissioned by the [Spa]nish court.

[RI]MER, WILLIAM (1816–79). A [larg]ely self-taught American artist who

was about 44 years old and a practicing doctor before he seriously undertook sculpture. Almost ignored during his lifetime, his paintings as well as his sculptures have since won increasing recognition.

ROBERT, HUBERT (1733–1808). A French artist who painted typical ancient ruins of the sort he saw in Italy and southern France.

ROBINSON, THEODORE (1852–96). An American landscapist who lived largely in France, where he became friendly with Monet, an association which nudged Robinson into Impressionism.

RODIN, AUGUSTE (1840–1917). Outstanding French sculptor of the 19th century. In his own lifetime his work was deemed controversial, earning him both extravagant praise and condemnation.

ROMANO, GIULIO (1499–1546). The favorite pupil and assistant of Raphael. His work was very popular in the 16th and 17th centuries. His name is mentioned in Shakespeare's *A Winter's Tale*.

ROMNEY, GEORGE (1734–1802). Along with Reynolds and Gainsborough, one of the more successful British portraitists of the 18th century. All three artists tended to idealize their sitters while realizing a good likeness.

ROSA, SALVATOR (1615–73). An Italian poet, actor, and musician as well as a painter. His peopled landscapes, often dramatic and wild, strongly influenced the development of Romanticism in art.

ROSSETTI, DANTE GABRIEL (1828–82). A British artist and poet. Founding member of the Pre-Raphaelite Brotherhood, a group that protested what they considered the vulgar productions of the machine age. They hoped to restore and maintain the high standards of art and culture they believed had existed in the simpler days before Raphael brought Renaissance art to its climax.

ROSZAK, THEODORE (1907–81). A modern Polish-born American sculptor whose typical works are of metal forged into almost explosive, intricate symbolic designs.

ROTHKO, MARK (1903–70). See p. 105.

ROUAULT, GEORGES (1871–1958). See p. 97.

ROUSSEAU, HENRI (1844–1910).

The best known of the primitive French painters. Although he was self-taught and naive, the spontaneity of his work soon won the regard of very sophisticated artists of his time. In 1908 Picasso staged a banquet in his honor.

ROWLANDSON, THOMAS (1756–1827). One of the greatest British caricaturists and social commentators.

RUBENS, PETER PAUL (1577–1640). See p. 60.

RUISDAEL, JACOB VAN (1628–82). See p. 63.

RUSKIN, JOHN (1819–1900). A very influential British critic and author. In 1870 he became the first university professor of art.

RYDER, ALBERT PINKHAM (1847–1917). An eccentric and reclusive American romantic painter. The obscure, mystical visions depicted in his paintings are symbols of man's lonely struggle against the forces of nature.

SAINT-GAUDENS, AUGUSTUS (1848–1907). A towering figure in the American art world around the turn of the century. At that time Saint-Gaudens was generally considered this country's foremost sculptor.

SARGENT, JOHN SINGER (1856–1925). See p. 82.

SARTO, ANDREA DEL. See del Sarto, Andrea.

SASSETTA (STEFANO DI GIOVANNI, 1392–1450). An outstanding early Sienese painter whose work was still medieval in spirit at a time when artists in nearby Florence were cultivating the new ideals of the Renaissance.

SEBASTIANO DEL PIOMBO (SEBASTIANO VENEZIANO, 1485–1547). A friend of Michelangelo's, whose drawings he sometimes used for his own compositions. He was active mostly in Rome.

SEGONZAC, ANDRÉ DUNOYER DE (1884–1974). A French painter in the conservative tradition, which he interpreted in his own personal style.

SEURAT, GEORGES (1859–91). See p. 87.

SHAHN, BEN (1898–1969). See p. 103.

SHEELER, CHARLES (1883–1965). An American painter and photographer. Many of his works in both me-

dia celebrate the sharply designed patterns of industrial architecture, machinery, and folk artifacts. In his abstractions of reality Sheeler never obscured the essential identity of his models.

SHINN, EVERETT (1876–1953). A journalist and painter who for a while was a member of the Ashcan School. The subjects of much of his best and typical work were ballet dancers and stage entertainers.

SIGNAC, PAUL (1863–1935). An independent French painter whose style recalls Impressionism. His bright watercolors have a special appeal.

SIGNORELLI, LUCA (about 1441–1523). Probably studied with Piero della Francesca. Painted two frescoes in the Sistine Chapel and is noted for his influence on Piero di Cosimo and Michelangelo. His greatest work is a series of awesome paintings depicting the end of the world, scenes teeming with writhing, straining, anatomically detailed bodies.

SIQUEIROS, DAVID ALFARO (1898–1974). A famed Mexican muralist whose work is marked by Aztec influence. At times he used industrial paints and spray-gun techniques on outdoor walls. Also an easel painter and graphic artist, he was a political activist involved with trade unionism and was frequently jailed by the authorities.

SISLEY, ALFRED (1839–99). A French-born British Impressionist who for a while was strongly influenced by Monet.

SLOAN, JOHN (1871–1951). An important member of the Ashcan School. Many of his paintings are spirited and understanding studies of New York street scenes, executed in vigorous brushstrokes.

SMIBERT, JOHN (1688–1751). The first trained English painter to practice in the American colonies.

SMITH, DAVID (1906–65). See p. 101.

SOUTINE, CHAIM (1894–1943). See p. 97.

STEEN, JAN (1626–79). See p. 58.

STELLA, FRANK (1936–). See p. 105.

STIEGLITZ, ALFRED (1864–1946). An American photographer who played a very important part in introducing modern art to the American public and in encouraging modern American artists.

STUART, GILBERT (1755–1828). See p. 75.

SULLY, THOMAS (1783–1872). An English-born American artist who produced thousands of paintings, mostly portraits. In 1837 he went to England with a commission to paint a likeness of Queen Victoria. That added to his fame if not to his professional reputation.

TAMAYO, RUFINO (1899–   ). One of the best-known Mexican artists. His colorful paintings show his appreciation of pre-Columbian forms and popular native arts.

TENIERS THE YOUNGER, DAVID (1610–90). A Flemish painter best known for his tavern scenes, alchemists, and hermits. He and his assistants turned out a great many pictures of that sort for a ready market.

TER BORCH, GERARD (1617–81). A highly skilled Dutch painter of portraits and everyday scenes. He was influenced by Frans Hals and, after a trip to Spain, by Velázquez.

TIEPOLO, GIOVANNI BATTISTA (1696–1770). The most important Venetian painter and decorator of the 18th century. He was internationally famous and worked in other countries as well as in Italy. He spent the latter part of his life in Madrid, where he decorated the royal palace. His art was dazzlingly theatrical, produced with remarkable grace and what seems like effortless, sure technique.

TINTORETTO, JACOPO (1518–94). One of the great Renaissance artists in Venice. He particularly admired Titian's color and Michelangelo's drawing. His style was lyrical and dramatic. His boldly conceived subjects are often alive with movement and expressed emotion. The influence of his work can be seen in paintings by El Greco.

TITIAN (TIZIANO VECELLIO, 1477/87–1576). See p. 52.

TOBEY, MARK (1890–1976). An American abstract artist. After a visit to Shanghai and Japan, he sought to combine his visions of the Far East and the West, his free-form abstractions, and his study of eastern calligraphy.

TOULOUSE-LAUTREC, HENRI DE (1864–1901). See p. 89.

TRUMBULL, JOHN (1756–1843). An American portrait and historical painter who saw himself as chronicler of the American Revolution. In 1816 Congress commissioned him to paint panels of the Capitol's Rotunda.

TURNER, JOSEPH MALLORD WILLIAM (1775–1851). See p. 77.

TWACHTMAN, JOHN HENRY (1853–1902). One of the earliest American Impressionists. Studied in various European cities, notably in Paris. Using delicate colors thinly and broadly applied to the canvas, he evoked an image of the landscape instead of defining it.

UCCELLO, PAOLO (about 1396/97–1475). One of the earliest Florentine painters to master perspective and to formulate the Renaissance style.

UTRILLO, MAURICE (1883–1955). A French artist with a highly personal style who repeatedly painted moody views of the streets of suburban Paris.

VAN DER GOES, HUGO (about 1440–82). A famous Flemish painter with an individual style that ranks him among the finest artists of his time and place. He died in a monastery, haunted by occasional fits of insanity.

VANDERLYN, JOHN (1775–1852). The first American to go to Paris rather than to London for his training. The public was indifferent to the kinds of paintings he preferred to do. He died embittered and impoverished.

VAN DER WEYDEN, ROGIER (about 1400–64). One of the great masters of early Flemish painting. In his religious works he achieved a rare combination of passion and elegance. As a tribute to his genius, in about 1435 he was appointed City Painter of Bruges, a post created for him.

VAN DYCK, ANTHONY (1599–1641). See p. 60.

VAN EYCK, JAN (1380/90–1441). See p. 54.

VAN GOGH, VINCENT (1853–90). See p. 90.

VASARI, GIORGIO (1511–74). An Italian painter, architect, and writer. In 1550 he published *Lives of the Artists,* an important work in which he described the origins and development of Italian art and the lives of the painters who contributed to it.

VEDDER, ELIHU (1836–1923). An American painter and illustrator, best remembered for his illustrations for *The Rubaiyat* and for his murals in the Library of Congress.

VELÁZQUEZ, DIEGO RODRIGUEZ DE SILVA Y (1599–1660). See p. 64.

VERMEER, JAN (1632–75). See p. 59.

VERNET, CLAUDE JOSEPH (1714–89). The first important French landscapist after Poussin and Lorraine. Spent most of his life in Italy. His romantic marine paintings are typically of shipwrecks and storms.

VERONESE, PAOLO (1528–88). One of the important Venetian painters of the Renaissance. Noted for the clear, luminous coloring of his work and for his superb manner of rendering textures. His influence on Venetian painting remained strong during the century after his death.

VERROCCHIO, ANDREA DEL (1435–88). See p. 49.

VIGÉE-LEBRUN, ELIZABETH (1755–1842). The favorite portrait painter of Marie Antoinette in the years before the French Revolution.

VLAMINCK, MAURICE DE (1876–1958). A self-taught French artist, a printmaker as well as a painter. He was also an author, a musician, and a bicycle racer. One of the first artists to be influenced by African tribal sculpture.

VUILLARD, EDOUARD (1868–1940). See p. 91.

WATTEAU, JEAN-ANTOINE (1684–1721). See p. 69.

WEBER, MAX (1881–1961). A Russian-born American painter whose work became increasingly abstract in the decades before his death, having previously portrayed contemporary and social themes.

WEST, BENJAMIN (1738–1820). An American-born artist who went to England via Italy as a young man and never returned to his homeland. He became a close friend of King George III's. In 1792 he was elected president of the Royal Academy, succeeding Joshua Reynolds. His London studio was a virtual schoolroom for fellow Americans who came there in great numbers to study under him.

WEYDEN, ROGIER VAN DER. See Van der Weyden, Rogier.

WHISTLER, JAMES ABBOT McNEILL (1834–1903). See p. 82.

WOOD, GRANT (1892–1942). painter of the American Midwe With Thomas Hart Benton and Jo Steuart Curry, leading artists of t regional movements of the 193 Grant turned his back on the a vanced art of the time and chose represent the homespun qualities American life as he viewed it in t country's heartland. One of Woo best-known works, *American Goth* was intended as a satire, but has cor to be taken as a more serious ch acter study of two typical midweste Americans.

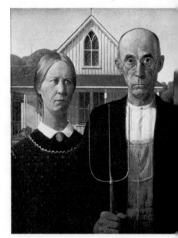

Grant Wood, *American Gothic,* 19

WRIGHT, FRANK LLOYD (186 1959). See p. 84.

WYETH, ANDREW NEWE (1917–   ). See p. 102.

ZORACH, WILLIAM (1887–19 A Lithuanian-born American sculp who worked largely in stone and wood. For the most part self-tau he became recognized as one of foremost American sculptors of day.

ZURBARÁN, FRANCISCO (1598–1664). A Spanish artist wh fame as a painter of monkish life v him the favor of the Spanish king. A celebrated for his superb still lifes, b as studies in themselves and as ba grounds for his figure paintings.